Kindle the Fire

His plans for you are good!

Blessings,
Jodi :)

JER. 29:11

Kindle the Fire

An Acts 29 Message

Jodi Marie Hicks

authorHOUSE®

AuthorHouse™
1663 Liberty Drive
Bloomington, IN 47403
www.authorhouse.com
Phone: 1-800-839-8640

Published by AuthorHouse   04/11/2013

ISBN: 978-1-4817-2172-1 (sc)
ISBN: 978-1-4817-2167-7 (hc)
ISBN: 978-1-4817-2171-4 (e)

Library of Congress Control Number: 2013903758

This book is printed on acid-free paper.

Foreword

On rare occasions, someone hears the call of God and is thoroughly obedient to that call. This, of course, always results in an expression of the heart of God that is clear, concise, and truly a blessing. Jodi has done just this in her new book, *Kindle the Fire*. In the following pages, you will find fresh and unique revelation into the book of Acts, intertwined with precious testimony from someone who has known life's challenges and continues to overcome. This tapestry of God's word and personal reflection will bring a greater understanding of the early church and the unsearchable riches that sustain us all. It will also issue a challenge to go deeper with the Bible and with prayer, resulting in the establishment of intimacy and identity. This book is truly anointed by the Holy Spirit and a gift to us all.

Dr. Rick Bass, M.D.
Pastor—Houston, Texas

Chapter Reviews

Chapter One: Chosen
"This chapter gets to the heart of being chosen by God—the foundation of what it means to walk with Him."

—*Thomas*

Chapter Two: Filled
"I am so thankful for the Holy Spirit! I became more aware that He is always there to guide me and fill me."

—*Virginia*

Chapter Three: Healed
"I am inspired to share my experiences as a cancer survivor with others who are in need of spiritual and physical healing."

—*Donna*

Chapter Four: Boldness
"Bring it, Jesus!"

—*Emily*

Chapter Five: Truth
"I have hope knowing that God is not looking for perfect people, just open honest hearts."

—*Rick*

Chapter Six: Faith
"This chapter ignited a fire in me to know more about faith and to seek God's heart regarding His version of faith for my life."

—*Sarah*

Chapter Seven: Witness
"I was provoked to think about my own daily witness for the Lord, and I became more conscious of the reality of being His temple."

—*Charlene*

Chapter Eight: Preach

"This chapter made me aware that it is not the quantity of your preaching of the gospel, but the quality that gets the message across."

—*Rich*

Chapter Nine: Vision

"I am inspired to ask God to let me see what He sees and to know His heart so I can do His will and not mine."

—*Femi*

Chapter Ten: Pray

"My eyes have been opened to the reality of what took place on the cross, and I am reminded of the Father's desire to hear my voice and respond to my prayers."

—*Megan*

Chapter Eleven: Grace

"Grace is God's power put into practice in my life, and it frees me so I can help free others."

—*Margit*

Chapter Twelve: Arise

"This chapter taught me the value of obedience, even in the midst of challenging circumstances."

—*Nathaniel*

Chapter Thirteen: Justified

"I have a better understanding of the love God has for me and for all who believe in Him; we are indeed justified by the greatest Justifier of all!"

—*Tommy*

Chapter Fourteen: Turn

"This has helped expose the reality of my justification, redemption, and grace and shown me how to protect it."

—*Keevon*

Chapter Fifteen: Conversion
"You write very smoothly, effectively, and sincerely."

—Steve

Chapter Sixteen: Servants
"I had a fresh reminder of how much my will must be fully surrendered to His will in order to be content."

—Dan

Chapter Seventeen: Offspring
"I received a key revelation from the Father: the establishment of true, familial intimacy within the hearts of His children. This is our identity! We are sons and daughters!"

—Bryan

Chapter Eighteen: Occupation
"This chapter wrecked me and completely renewed my mind regarding the work I do."

—Esther

Chapter Nineteen: Miracles
"We are called to live as ambassadors of God, and this instilled a fire in me to release Jesus into my community!"

—Christopher

Chapter Twenty: Purchased
"This chapter is very good theology made quite simple and effective."
—Tom

Chapter Twenty-One: Disciple
"I am reminded that God has powerful things in store for my life and that I should seize every opportunity to act in His love."

—Noah

Chapter Twenty-Two: Testimony
"This chapter has helped me to see that verbal communication adds significant impact to the message that Jesus Christ is the Lord of life."

—Allen

Chapter Twenty-Three: Cheer
"This was an instrument used by God to speak to me during a difficult trial in my life."

—*Stephanie*

Chapter Twenty-Four: Hope
"I have been inspired by this chapter to be certain in the things I hope for in Christ because that certainty is what makes the unseen become seen."

—*Vanessa*

Chapter Twenty-Five: Jesus
"I am amazed by how smart God is—that He could take Jesus and make Him dirty with my sin so He could make me forgiven, righteous, and white as snow."

—*Stephen*

Chapter Twenty-Six: Inheritance
"I am Royalty! I forget it. Thank you so much for the reminder!"

—*Diane*

Chapter Twenty-Seven: Believe
"My spirit has been stirred to remember that I have favor to do what God has called me to do, in spite of the obstacles that come my way, if I will only believe."

—*Roberta*

Chapter Twenty-Eight: Fire
"I was greatly encouraged to shake off attacks, suffer no harm, and believe that my trials will be used by my Father in heaven to minister His love to the very people who attack me."

—*Daniel*

First Fruits

Abba, this book is Yours.
And every book that follows.
Thank You for kindling my fire.
May it burn for You all of my days.
Be exalted.

Dedication

Mom,
All of the books in the world could not contain my gratitude.
The love of God and the heart of a servant flow through you
in miraculous ways. You inspire me *beyond* words.
I love you so.

Grandma Dolly,
If I can touch a fraction of the lives you did with your
compassion and commitment, my life will be complete.
Thank you for everything. I pray that this book takes
flight and finds itself in your heavenly hands.
You are greatly loved and missed by all.

"YAY GOD!"

Acknowledgments

Holy Spirit, You are the true Author. Thank You for being my counselor, guide, and friend every step of the way. Apart from You, I can do nothing.

Heaven only knows the countless number of people who have prayed me through the process of writing my first book. Friends and family members scattered around the globe have encouraged, supported, and inspired me. I want to begin by thanking the faithful Ring of Fire Editing Team. Without you, this project would be incomplete. You gave your heart, prayers, time, talent, and attention to this book. I am forever grateful. I also appreciate every person who jumped on board the Social Media Prayer Train to pray for me. G'Mama and Granddaddy, thank you so much for your powerful prayers and many blessings, including access to my perfect, peaceful writer's nook with a view! Mike, thank you for your prayerful artistic perspective and for donating the cover design. Your tireless commitment to serve the Lord with your gifts is truly an inspiration. Rick, I am so grateful for that limb you found yourself on time and time again. Your encouragement, prayers, and wisdom have carried me. Emily, you are a gem. Thank you for the spontaneous worship and much needed laughter. It sustained me. Oh, and Noah, thank you for changing my Facebook and Twitter passwords. Enough said. To all of my ministry partners, brothers and sisters in Christ, and spiritual mothers and fathers—I pray that you are honored and blessed by the seeds you have sown and the fruit of your labor. I love you all!

Finally, to Watty Piper, the author who first inspired me as a child . . . "*I think I can! I think I can!*" Thank you for the reminder.

"I can do all things through Christ who strengthens me."
Philippians 4:13

From the Author

I love road trips. It has always been easy for me to jump in my car and take off on some unplanned excursion. No expectations, only a desire to seek and discover. Regardless of where the road leads me, I have never returned home without a greater understanding of who I am and why I am here. I want to invite you to take a little trip with me. To a place you have not been before. I encourage you to remain open to whatever lies ahead. Oh, and travel light! Carry only hope and anticipation with you. You may be surprised at how this adventure turns out.

It is no accident that you are reading this. Your Father in heaven has you on His heart and mind. I have prayed for you from the moment I wrote the very first word. God wants to introduce Himself to you in new and powerful ways. He has a great plan and purpose for your life. He wants you to know who *He* says you are. My prayer is that this book will take you on a journey into the beautiful, compassionate, tender heart of God. As you read, I pray that you will grow in intimacy with the One who loves you more than life. I pray that you will discover your true identity and find healing for your soul. I pray that you will be encouraged, empowered, and enabled to pursue your dreams. I pray that you will be inspired and motivated to make a difference. I pray that you will be convicted and convinced by a loving Father that He is more than enough for your every need. I pray that you will hunger and thirst for God's word and His presence. I pray that your heart will be set ablaze by Love and that you will have a burning desire to share Him with others.

We will never fully know God, but we have been given an amazing opportunity to seek Him all the days of our lives. Expect Him to meet you in the pages ahead. Let *His* words move your heart, fill your soul, and change your life forever. Determine to know Him more every day. Soften your heart and prepare to receive from Him. He will whisper to you in the stillness.

Enjoy the journey,

Jodi Marie

Contents

Introduction

The Boot Camp Bible Study Series™ was birthed out of my desire to help others grow in their understanding and knowledge of God's word. I began to facilitate online Boot Camp Bible Studies in 2006 and eventually organized Boot Camp Bible Study groups in various locations with people who were hungry and thirsty for more of God in their lives.

Why is this series called Boot Camp? By definition, boot camp is a military training camp for new recruits. It is a focused time of preparation, discipline, and submission. Over the years, God has acquired my attention in very specific ways through seasons of intense training that I have affectionately referred to as "Boot Camp Seasons." Each season varies according to my spiritual needs and God's plans for my life, but there are always great lessons to be learned and new skills to be obtained. I often feel like a soldier being equipped for battle.

The Boot Camp Bible Study Series™ is designed to provoke hearts to greater intimacy with God through the study of His word. Each Bible Study/Devotional is unique. The Boot Camp Badge (located on the back cover of each book in the series) identifies the number of days or weeks covered by the study, along with the primary focus of the study.

The Bible is inexhaustible. The purpose of this series is to help you stay engaged with God's word and His ways on a daily basis. This book is not intended to replace the Holy Bible, rather to be an accompanying study aid and devotional. It is personal and intentional in its approach to lead you closer to the heart of God, discovering your identity in Him every step of the way.

Kindle the Fire: An Acts 29 Message is a divine invitation to pick up where the book of Acts leaves off in Chapter 28. It will challenge and encourage you to pursue God wholeheartedly. It will help you understand who you are and why you are here. It will teach you to live with passion and purpose with the help of the Holy Spirit. It will inspire you to grow, stretch you beyond your comfort zone, and remind you that you can do all things through Christ who strengthens you.[1] It is a radical clarion call to all who want to experience and encounter more of God in their lives.

This particular study focus is "28 Days of Identification." Each day you are encouraged to read one chapter in the Bible from the book of Acts, followed by the corresponding chapter in *Kindle the Fire*. The goal is to spend time meditating on God's word and practically applying it to your life daily.

The title page for each chapter includes a specific word that was selected from the related chapter of Acts. The only exception is Chapter 5. The title of Chapter 5 is not actually found in Acts 5, but it epitomizes the message. Below the English word is the Greek word that was originally used in early Biblical manuscripts. It is written in Greek lettering, followed by the English spelling and pronunciation. Below that is the definition of the Greek word. Words often lose much of their meaning in translation. Studying earlier texts enables a more accurate understanding of the word of God. The New King James Version of the Bible is used throughout this study to maintain consistency.

There are also interactive and contemplative pages at the end of each chapter. Following is an explanation of the sections on those pages:

Pause and Reflect
Take some time to consider the questions and statements in this section. A journaling area is available to record your thoughts.

Raw and Real
One sentence tells the truth about where the church (the *ekklesia*—the *people*, not the *premises*) is today compared to where the church of Acts was.

Short and Sweet
Pray this brief prayer at the end of each chapter. Add your own thoughts and requests as well.

---

[1]   Philippians 4:13

Meditate and Memorize

Each chapter highlights a scripture that encompasses the daily message. Meditate on it and memorize it if you so desire. Joshua 1:8 says, "This Book of the Law shall not depart from your mouth, but you shall meditate in it day and night, that you may observe to do according to all that is written in it. For then you will make your way prosperous, and then you will have good success." Meditation is the key to having God's word written on your heart. Talk to Him about the Scriptures, ask Him questions, and apply His word to your life.

Believe and Receive

This is a concise statement of affirmation related to the chapter. Confess and repeat it throughout the day. Believe that it is true and receive it into your heart.

Listen and Learn

This section allows you to communicate with God through prayer and writing. Consistent journaling provides an opportunity to express what is on your heart and mind, while connecting intimately with your Father in heaven. Relationship is a two-way street. Sometimes we talk, and sometimes we listen. God has something to say to you. *Learn to listen and listen to learn.*

Create and Relate

There is a blank page at the end of each chapter. Use it to connect with God creatively. Genesis 1:1 says, "In the beginning God created . . . ." In the Bible, God reveals Himself first as Creator. You are made in His image and likeness. Grab your pencils, pens, and crayons. Draw, design, and doodle whatever you desire. Is there a picture or a vision you want to capture? Articulate it through art. Attach a photograph to the page or create a collage. Write a poem or a song. Be creative, like the God who created you.

The book of Acts is a fascinating adventure through the lives of the men and women who established the early church. We can learn a great deal both individually and corporately from those who have gone before us. They maintained a burning love and zeal for God, even in the most challenging of circumstances. They understood their identity, they feared God more than man, and they set the world on fire for His glory.

Your identity encompasses your individuality, personality, character, and uniqueness. Discovering your true identity does not happen overnight. It is a process that takes time and persistence. Dig deep as you read. Ask questions of God and others. Search the Scriptures for yourself. Disagree with me if you must, but *own* your identity and faith. Know *why* you believe *what* you believe. Do not merely trust tradition. Do not borrow someone else's core values. Do not depend on another person's faith to sustain you. Take the journey for yourself and discover who *God* says you are.

I encourage you to stop periodically throughout this study and do a heart check. Are you growing? Are you communicating with the Holy Spirit on a regular basis? Are you being transformed by the renewing of your mind? The purpose of this book is to help you engage with God on a more personal level. Sometimes this requires potentially uncomfortable moments of silence in His presence, gazing into your own heart and soul. It is there that you will begin to understand who you really are. In the stillness, you will know.

"Be still, and know that I am God."
Psalm 46:10

ACTS 1
DAY ONE

CHOSEN

ἐκλέγομαι

eklegomai

ek-leg'-om-ahee

to select;
pick one out of many

If you are holding this book in your hands, you have been invited to go deeper in your relationship with God. You have an opportunity to discover and affirm your identity in Him in a greater way. What exactly does it mean to be chosen by God? Why does the God of the universe, the Father of creation, the all-knowing Being who dwells in eternal glory call you and I "chosen?"

First and foremost, you are chosen to be in a real, loving relationship with your Father in heaven. You are chosen to walk with Him and enjoy Him. You are chosen to worship Him and live out His will. You are chosen for a purpose, not to promote self, but to link arms with other purpose-filled believers and bring God's kingdom to earth in every sphere of society. It is only from the place of intimacy with God that you can accomplish all that He has created and chosen you to do. Everything you are purposed to be should flow from loving communion with your Creator.

Matthew 22:14 says, "For many are called, but few are chosen." Many are called to salvation. However, few accept this invitation to intimacy with God and live accordingly. Few truly understand the imputed righteousness of Christ and the sanctification of the Spirit that lead to real encounter and relationship with God. The chosen child of God is one who makes a decision to live obediently and intimately with Him moment by moment, surrendering and forsaking all for Him, and opting to pursue a holy life for His glory. This is evident in the lives of many of the men and women in the book of Acts.

The word *chosen* is used twice in the first chapter of Acts, and both times it refers to being *selected by God for a purpose.* Acts 1:2 says that Jesus ". . . through the Holy Spirit had given commandments to the apostles whom He had chosen . . . ." Have you ever paused to consider why He chose those particular twelve men to establish His kingdom

> *"For many are called, but few are chosen."*
>
> *Matthew 22:14*

2

on earth? What was so special about them? Regardless of their occupation, education, or experience, I believe Jesus chose them because He knew that they would say yes to His call. He knew that they would be willing to walk with Him daily. The beauty of saying yes to Jesus is that He knows of what you are fully capable. There should be no hesitation when you hear His invitation to "Follow Me." Your Creator knows you better than you know yourself, and His plans for you are good.[2]

In Acts 1:24-25, the disciples were gathered together in prayer in the upper room to choose a replacement for Judas. They prayed, "You, O Lord, who know the hearts of all, show which of these two You have chosen to take part in this ministry and apostleship from which Judas by transgression fell, that he might go to his own place." God reveals throughout His word that He has chosen certain people for specific purposes. Once that purpose is identified, however, it is up to us to lean into Him and fulfill it. The disciples, for example, were chosen to take the gospel to the nations. They were used by God to lead others into His presence. They consistently kindled fires in cold, wounded, captive hearts. They healed bodies and performed miracles by the Spirit and power of God. They truly set the world on fire after spending three years establishing a close, personal relationship with Jesus. You and I are no different. God has chosen us and called us His own. He wants to use us to bring heaven to earth, but everything we do must be done from the place of intimacy with Him. John 15:5 says, "I am the vine, you are the branches. He who abides in Me, and I in him, bears much fruit; for without Me you can do nothing."

Your Creator knows you better than you know yourself, and His plans for you are good.

Every person on the face of this earth was created for a reason. When you begin to understand that your life has meaning, as those in the book of Acts did, you will live differently. Your purpose is not independent of your passion,

[2]   Jeremiah 29:11

3

and passionate people cause things to shift in the atmosphere around them. There is a spark inside of you that was placed there by God to ignite a fire in the earth that will bring glory to His name. When you live in the fullness of your destiny as a chosen child of God, you will experience a life of complete satisfaction in Him that you were designed to desire.

There will never be a void that cannot be filled by God as you pursue greater intimacy with your Creator. There is a deep sense of belonging that comes from knowing that you have been handpicked, called out, and set apart for something special. There is great comfort in believing that your life is not an accident. There is tremendous hope in the realization that destiny awaits you. There is excitement and anticipation in discovering that you were created to make a difference. You were not a last resort in the mind of God. You are cherished and important. A Majestic Artist painted the canvas of your life with beauty and intention. He loves you powerfully, passionately, purposefully, and eternally.

Regardless of how terrible life's circumstances may seem at times, you still have breath in your lungs because God is not finished with you yet. There is so much more He wants to teach you about Himself and about the infinite reasons why He chose you. With His help, you will do something great in your lifetime, but you must also remember that God defines greatness. As you pursue Him and His plans for your life, view your "great" destiny through the eyes of God rather than through the eyes of man or through the lens of a striving, performance-based culture.

The first chapter of Acts reveals some of the facets and benefits of being chosen by God. As you read the following italicized phrases, make them personal and allow God to speak to you about what it means to be "chosen." In verse 3, Jesus *presented Himself alive* to the disciples and *spoke to them* about things pertaining to the Kingdom. In verse 4, He was *in the midst of the assembly*, and He *gave them instructions.* In verse 5, He *foretold the future* and *restored their hope.* In verse 7, He *answered their questions.* In verse 8, He *encouraged them* and *revealed their purpose.* In verse 9, He *demonstrated His supernatural power.* In verse 10, He *sent heavenly messengers* to them in His absence. Oh, the perks of being a chosen child of God!

It is important to note that the chosen ones had responsibilities as well. In verse 10, they *looked steadfastly toward heaven.* In verse 14, they *gathered together in unity and prayer.* Finally, in verse 24, they *acknowledged that God ordained certain people to accomplish specific tasks.* Once you accept that God has chosen you, you will need to do your part to see that His plans are fulfilled in your life. There is no magic formula, but we can learn a lot from the way the disciples walked out their faith. They fixed their eyes on Jesus (Acts 1:10, Hebrews 12:2), they did not forsake the gathering of the brethren (Acts 1:14, Hebrews 10:25), they lived in unity (Acts 1:14, 1 Peter 3:8), and they communicated often with God through prayer (Acts 1:14, 1 Thessalonians 5:17).

Being chosen means that you are gifted in certain areas to do something unique in this earth that no one else can do. You have a DNA, fingerprint, heartbeat, voice pattern, and eye print that will never be duplicated. You are the only *you* that will ever exist. The unique identity of mankind reveals the Creator's desire to connect personally and individually with His children. God has something special for you to do in this life that will be birthed through your intimate pursuit of Him. Do you know what it is? Allow me to remind you that you are a one-of-a-kind masterpiece. You have the signature of a perfect, holy God inscribed into your spirit, soul, and body. Nothing will be impossible for you if you will only believe.

God loves all of His children with an everlasting love. There is nothing you could say or do to make Him love you any less. He is your biggest fan! He is cheering for you in the midst of every storm. He weeps when you weep, and He celebrates your victories with all of the hosts of heaven. He delights in you, He calls you Beloved, and He longs to see you become *all* that He created you to be. His dreams for your life are greater than anything you could ask or think or imagine. His love for you can never be earned or lost. It is eternal. You are worthy of His best, and you are valued by Him every second of every day. In fact,

He loves you so much that He sent His Son to die for your sins so you can live in complete freedom from all condemnation, fear, shame, and doubt.

This life is not a dress rehearsal. It is the real deal, and you have been given one shot to make the best of it. You will not always get it right. In fact, expect to make some major mistakes along the way. Jesus already made provision for that through His blood. When you fall, just pick yourself up, dust yourself off, and repent of your sins. Then move forward with perseverance, faith, and tenacity. God is with you *always*. He *cannot* fail, and neither can you as long as you let Him lead. Even in the midst of your greatest trials and biggest messes, there is a way out. Do not allow discouragement to keep you from finishing the race.

You have been chosen for greatness because you serve a great God! You are not just another number, and you are *never* forgotten. You are on the Father's heart all day every day, and He cares about every detail of your life. Keep your chin up and know that you are not alone. You have been chosen by the Alpha and the Omega, the One who knows the end before the beginning. His plans for you are glorious, and His will is that you live on purpose with an abiding knowledge of His perfect love and power. Let it begin today.

> *God loves all of His children with an everlasting love. There is nothing you could say or do to make Him love you any less.*

Pause and Reflect

How will the revelation of being "chosen" by God change your relationship with Him and others?

_____

_____

_____

_____

_____

_____

_____

_____

_____

_____

_____

Raw and Real

The enemy has lied to God's children and prevented them from discovering their true identity.

Short and Sweet

Loving God, I want to grow in my relationship with You. I want to know who *You* say I am. Thank You for choosing me. Reveal Your great purpose for my life and help me fulfill it for Your glory. Amen.

Meditate and Memorize

"And they prayed and said 'You, O Lord, who know the hearts of all, show which of these two You have chosen to take part in this ministry and apostleship from which Judas by transgression fell, that he might go to his own place.'"
—Acts 1:24-25

Believe and Receive

God picked me.

Listen and Learn
Talk to God about intimacy and purpose.

_____
_____
_____
_____
_____
_____
_____
_____
_____
_____
_____
_____
_____
_____
_____
_____
_____
_____
_____
_____
_____
_____
_____
_____
_____
_____
_____
_____
_____

Create and Relate
Use this space to connect with God through creativity.

ACTS 2
DAY TWO

FILLED

πληρόω

plēroō

play-ro'-o

to cram, furnish, satisfy, or execute;
to finish or accomplish;
to perfect or complete;
to cause to abound;
to supply liberally

Practically speaking, to be *filled* means that something is no longer empty. It refers to a particular vessel containing a specific substance, typically to nearly overflowing. That is exactly what God wants for you. He wants to fill you with His Holy Spirit in such a way that you are empowered to live a life of overflowing abundance and victory.

Imagine for a moment that you have an empty glass in front of you. Now place as many rocks in your imaginary glass as you can possibly fit into it. Is it full? Some would say yes. However, if you place sand on top of your imaginary rocks, you will notice that it slowly trickles down into the empty spaces in the glass. Now is it full? Not exactly. Imagine again that you are gently pouring water into your glass that seems to already be "filled" with rocks and sand. As you pour the water into the glass, you notice that it begins to saturate the sand, compressing it, and making more room for a substance that you originally did not imagine your glass could contain. God wants to fill you up the same way. He does not want even the most microscopic spaces to remain empty in your life.

God alone is completely aware of the cracks and crevices that need to be filled in your soul. He sees where your spirit is dry and could use a little water. In fact, when you think you are full, God says, "I see room for a little more." Acts 2:2 says, "And suddenly there came a sound from heaven, as of a rushing mighty wind, and it filled the whole house where they were sitting." God wants to fill your whole house, your entire temple—spirit, soul, and body. The problem with today's grab-and-go society is that many people are "rocking" along, building their lives on sinking "sand," and saving little room for the refreshing, healing "water" of God's word and presence. Hebrews 4:12 says, "For the word of God is living and powerful, and sharper than any two-edged sword, piercing even to the division of soul and spirit, and of joints and marrow, and is a discerner of the thoughts and intents of the heart." In other words, the word of God flows like the water in your imaginary glass into the places that you cannot see with your naked eye, transforming you and filling you in every way.

Acts 2 is a perfect picture of what it means to be filled with the Holy Spirit. Apart from the presence and power of the Holy Spirit operating in and through us, we cannot walk in our true identity in Christ, individually or corporately. It is His indwelling Spirit who leads us into all truth, comforts us in our times of need, satisfies our deepest longings, and empowers us to fulfill our destinies. Apart from Him, we can do nothing.[3]

> *When you think you are full, God says, "I see room for a little more."*

God is holy. Holiness is an aspect of His character that is expressed thoroughly and repeatedly throughout Scripture. When mankind's carnal nature leads him astray, it is the conviction and beauty of the *Holy* Spirit that will provoke him to look more like God.

I invited God into my life in a fresh way through the baptism of the Holy Spirit in 2007, less than eighteen months after I became a born-again Christian. The word of God describes two baptisms, the first with water and the second with fire. John the Baptist spoke about this in Matthew 3:11 when he said, "I indeed baptize you with water unto repentance, but He who is coming after me is mightier than I, whose sandals I am not worthy to carry. He will baptize you with the Holy Spirit and fire." Later, as the disciples were awaiting "the Promise of the Father" that Jesus spoke of in Acts 1:4, the Bible says, "Then there appeared to them divided tongues, as of fire, and one sat upon each of them. And they were all filled with the Holy Spirit and began to speak with other tongues, as the Spirit gave them utterance."[4]

This "Promise" that Jesus spoke of was not just a slight misting of His presence. It was a radical holy encounter with fire! It transformed the lives of the disciples and caused them to move forward in supernatural power. It created a burning desire within them to preach the gospel, heal the sick, raise the dead, and set the captives free according to the Great

---

[3] John 15:5

[4] Acts 2:3-4

13

Commission Jesus had given them.[5] The Holy Spirit filled them with such boldness and courage that many of them relentlessly followed Christ even unto their brutal deaths.

It must be clarified that water baptism is an outward expression of an inner faith. We are submerged in water to symbolically declare a washing away of the old sinful nature and a birthing of the new creation.[6] Then, through the baptism of fire, we are immersed in His Spirit and filled with His presence. The refining power of the Holy Spirit activated in your life will burn out every impurity and cause love to abound in supernatural ways. The book of Acts reveals that sometimes these two baptisms are separate events and other times they occur simultaneously.

The Greek poet and physician, Nicander, who lived approximately 200 years before Christ, described the process of making pickles using the Greek words *bapto* and *baptizo*. Nicander said that in order to make a pickle, the vegetable must first be dipped (*bapto*) in water then baptized (*baptizo*) in a vinegar solution. The first produces temporary change. The latter produces a new creation. This is the baptism of the Holy Spirit. It invokes permanent transformation in the life of a believer, ultimately causing a cucumber Christian to become a powerful pickle! A pickle will outlast a cucumber every time. Think about it. This is the will of God for all of His children.

The Holy Spirit is the third *person* of the godhead who was sent to empower each of us to do the greater works Jesus commands us to do.[7] With that empowerment comes a willingness to obey His word, a desire to be in the center of His perfect will, and a longing to grow in intimacy with Him. The fiery love and presence of His Spirit will smooth out the rough edges and make all the wrongs right. He will heal every hurt if (and only if) you will surrender to His perfect leadership. Trust that His ways are higher and better than your own.[8] As you do,

---

[5]   Mark 16:14-18

[6]   2 Corinthians 5:17

[7]   John 14:12

[8]   Isaiah 55:9

He will refine and purify your spirit, soul, and body, and He is guaranteed to get all of the glory.

When you allow the Holy Spirit to be large and in charge in your life, you will be amazed at what He is capable of doing in and through you. You will find that you are able to be content in plenty and content in lack. You will discover new gifts and abilities that you did not know you possessed. There will be evidence of His presence in the way you speak, act, and live. Others will notice a difference, and you will begin to understand the meaning of being a foreigner in a strange land.[9]

In the book of Acts, we are given a bird's-eye view into the daily lives of those who were truly filled with the power and love of God through His Holy Spirit. They performed miracles that would cause today's scientists to balk. They spoke with an authority that set the captives free. They stood before kings and shared the gospel. They even died joyfully and willingly for their beliefs. This is the evidence of the Holy Spirit in operation in the lives of born-again believers. *The Acts of the Apostles* (often referred to as *The Acts of the Holy Spirit*) is a snapshot of what it means to be a Spirit-filled believer. When you read the book of Acts, it will inspire you to take your walk with God to a new level. It is a historical account of truth in action. It is the *demonstration* of faith that is so necessary in a lost and dying world. We can learn a lot from those who have gone before us and prepared the way.

So what exactly happens when you are filled with the Holy Spirit? Acts 2 gives us clear insight into what it really means to be *filled*. Pay attention to the following effects on the disciples and the church as a result of being filled with the Holy Spirit. Allow God to speak to you personally about the importance of receiving all that He has for you.

After the disciples were filled with the Holy Spirit in Acts 2, they began to speak with other tongues (vs. 4). Others who witnessed the transformation were amazed and perplexed (vs. 7). They declared the wonderful works of God (vs. 11). People marveled at the supernatural evidence of God in their lives (vs. 12). Peter was empowered to boldly and courageously proclaim

---

[9]   1 Peter 2:11-12

the truth (vs. 14). The multitudes were saved and set free (vs. 41) and many wonders and signs were done (vs. 43).

As a result of the radical individual fires that were ignited in the hearts of the believers, the church also began to prosper corporately. Thousands were baptized (vs. 41). They gathered willingly and regularly to fellowship and pray (vs. 42). Extravagant giving and selflessness were commonplace (vs. 45). They enjoyed unity and worship (vs. 46), and they had favor with all the people (vs. 47). I simply cannot, for the life of me, figure out why anyone would deny the presence and power of the Holy Spirit! Who doesn't want to live like that?!

During his sermon in Acts 2:17-18, Peter referenced a passage of Scripture from the book of Joel: "And it shall come to pass in the last days, says God, that I will pour out of My Spirit on all flesh; your sons and your daughters shall prophesy, your young men shall see visions, your old men shall dream dreams. And on My menservants and on My maidservants I will pour out My Spirit in those days; and they shall prophesy."[10] The phrase, "pour out," literally means to spill forth, gush out, or bestow. It refers to God pouring out *Himself*. The Hebrew word for Spirit in that passage is *rûach*. It is His wind, the very breath and life of God. When you are filled with His Holy Spirit, God breathes the essence of who He is into your being. You will begin to encounter Him in new ways. You will be refined, refreshed, revived, and restored by His holy presence abiding within you.

Remember that God never changes.[11] His promises for the believers 2,000 years ago are also His promises for you today. God wants to pour Himself out and fill you to overflowing. Do not grieve Him by placing boundaries on what you allow Him to do in your life. Do not box Him in. *Take your leash off of the Creator*

> *You will be amazed at what He is capable of doing in and through you.*

---

[10] Joel 2:28-32
[11] Malachi 3:6

of the universe. Do not try to comprehend or understand His supernatural ways with your finite mind.

Hebrews 11:6 reminds us, "But without faith it is impossible to please Him, for he who comes to God must believe that He is, and that He is a rewarder of those who diligently seek Him." The Holy Spirit is God's great Promise and Reward for all who diligently seek Him. Let your faith arise and be *filled* with Him in a fresh way today. Then watch as your life begins to look a lot more like the book of Acts. We need Spirit-*filled* believers to pick up where this incredible book leaves off if we are going to become the Acts 29 church. Invite the Holy Spirit to fill you now.

Pause and Reflect

Consider the radical difference in the lives of the disciples after they were filled with the Holy Spirit.

_____
_____
_____
_____
_____
_____
_____
_____
_____
_____

Raw and Real

The Body of Christ is not operating in the full power and authority God has promised.

Short and Sweet

Holy Spirit, forgive me for the times I have grieved, suppressed, denied, rejected, or ignored you. Come fill me with Your power and presence today and help me live a life that glorifies You. Amen.

Meditate and Memorize

"And suddenly there came a sound from heaven, as of a rushing mighty wind, and it filled the whole house where they were sitting."
—Acts 2:2

Believe and Receive

God wants to fill me with Himself.

Listen and Learn
Dialogue with the Holy Spirit.

_____

_____

_____

_____

_____

_____

_____

_____

_____

_____

_____

_____

_____

_____

_____

_____

_____

_____

_____

_____

_____

_____

_____

_____

_____

_____

_____

_____

_____

_____

_____

_____

_____

_____

_____

_____

_____

Create and Relate
Use this space to connect with God through creativity.

ACTS 3
DAY THREE

HEALED

ἰάομαι

iaomai

ee-ah'-om-ahee

to cure;
make whole

You and I are really no different than the lame man in the third chapter of Acts. Everyone is dealing with something that is inoperable in his or her life at any given moment. Perhaps it is a physical disability or infirmity, but it could also be a spiritual void or an emotional battle. Maybe it is a dysfunction in your family or finances. The simple truth is that no one is exempt from tests and trials in this life. We have all heard the saying, "What doesn't kill you will only make you stronger." I would like to add to that an adage from a wise pastor I know: "Don't GO through it, GROW through it." Each time you allow God to put His holy, healing finger on a lame area of your life, you will grow closer to Him and grow stronger in your faith. Every weakness is a divine opportunity for God to reveal His absolute strength.

I love the irony of the lame man being healed at the gate called Beautiful in Acts 3:1-10. This first documented miracle of healing in the book of Acts could have occurred anywhere in Jerusalem, but the Lord, in His infinite love and wisdom, allowed it to occur at this particular gate of the temple for a reason. The Greek word for "Beautiful" in that passage of Scripture is *hōraios.* It means *belonging to the right hour or season; timely; flourishing.* The lame man was carried daily to this specific gate to ask for alms. In historical contexts, "alms" refers to money or food given out of compassion and mercy to poor people. This man was a beggar. He was desperate. He had a need and was not ashamed to admit it. He was a prime target for the power of God to be revealed when John and Peter arrived at the temple that day to pray. At the right time, in the right hour and season, he would flourish through the healing touch of a loving Savior.

> *Every weakness is a divine opportunity for God to reveal His absolute strength.*

Notice something about this scenario. A lame man lies begging at the temple. By today's standards, many people would turn a blind eye or a deaf ear to such a person. I have often witnessed people shunning the poor and the homeless. I am so grateful that we serve a God who meets our needs. Even when those around us seem to fail us, God will never abandon us or forsake us.[12] All He needed was two faithful servants who would obey His command to heal the sick and one disabled man who was "expecting to receive."[13] As a result, there was an encounter that would radically and eternally impact many lives. The rest is history.

As you continue to discover who you are in Christ, there are some miraculous healings that God wants to perform. He wants to make you whole in every area of your life—spirit, soul, and body. He wants you to be delivered from every stronghold and set free from all bondage. He wants you to be healthy and well in your physical body as well as in your emotions. He wants you to have the mind of Christ, and He wants your spiritual identity to be rooted and grounded in His love. Decades of living in a dark and sinful world will pollute the very best of men and women. There is a cleansing that God wants to do. He looks at your lame areas and prophetically calls them *"Beautiful."* He hears your request for alms, and He says, "I see a greater need!"

Like the lame man at the temple gate, many people ask for merely enough to get by as they live hopelessly and helplessly in a depravity or infirmity. What man sees as impossible and deems himself unworthy of, God sees as an opportunity to reveal His great love and compassion. He sees an open door to glorify His Son who died so that *all* may be healed through *faith* in His name. Your loving Father gazes on your imperfections and sees perfection. He makes no mistakes. You are His beloved child, and He calls you Beautiful. He wants to heal and restore everything the enemy has stolen from you since the day you were born. Do you believe?

So how can you "rise up and walk" as the lame man did? What did he do to get healed? First, it is important to know that you cannot "earn" God's love or healing. The love of God never changes. It is everlasting and eternal. His desire to make you whole is constant. In John 5:6, Jesus asked the man who had an infirmity for thirty-eight years, "Do you want to be made well?" Expounding on that from the Greek, the implication is that you

---

12   Deuteronomy 31:8
13   Acts 3:5

must *desire* and *choose* to be well in your spirit, soul, and body. In other words, Jesus wants to heal those who *want* to be healed.

The lame man in Acts 3 was determined. Even if he was having a bad day or a pity party, he allowed some friends to carry him to the gate *by faith*. He believed that he would get what he needed to survive. The great news is that God does not want you to merely *survive*. He wants you to *thrive*! He wants you to get a *testimony* out of your *test*! He wants others to look at your weakness and see *His* strength. He wants Jesus to get the glory from your healing.

> *"Do you want to be made well?"*
>
> *John 5:6*

Several avenues of healing are expressed throughout the Bible. Isaiah 53:5 says, "But He was wounded for our transgressions, He was bruised for our iniquities; the chastisement for our peace was upon Him, and by His stripes we are healed." 1 John 3:8 says, "For this purpose the Son of God was manifested, that He might destroy the works of the devil." The blood of Jesus was shed for your healing. Faith in Him alone will heal you. Other methods include: meditating on, believing in, and declaring aloud the words and promises of God; laying on of hands; receiving Holy Communion; anointing with oil; fasting and prayer. I would like to add that a positive mental attitude, good nutrition, exercise, and laughter are ways that you can *maintain* your healing. Healthy relationships and a life lived on purpose are also critical aspects of being made whole. We are triune beings—spirit, soul, and body. We must be wise stewards of all that God has entrusted to us. Today is a great day to begin taking better care of yourself, while believing God to heal you from the inside out.

Acts 10:38 tells us, ". . . God anointed Jesus of Nazareth with the Holy Spirit and with power, who went about doing good and healing all who were oppressed by the devil, for God was with Him." Jesus healed *all*. Matthew 8:16-17 says, "When evening had come, they brought to Him many who were demon-possessed. And He cast out the spirits with a word, and healed all who were sick, that it might be fulfilled which was spoken by Isaiah the prophet, saying: 'He Himself took our infirmities and bore our sicknesses.'" Again, He healed *all*. Acts 5:16 reveals that same anointing and power to heal: "Also a multitude gathered from the surrounding cities to Jerusalem, bringing sick people and those who were tormented by unclean spirits, and they were all healed." They were *all* healed by the power of Christ operating through faith-filled people like you and me.

God desires to partner with you to release His healing power to those in need. The principle of reaping and sowing applies here. If you need healing, sow healing into someone else's life. Unfortunately, many people are not being healed because Spirit-filled believers are not operating in their full authority and obeying the voice of God. The Holy Spirit will whisper His desire to heal people to those who have asked Him to use them. Then it is up to us to do our part. God is fully able to supernaturally heal His children without any intervention from us at all. However, He chooses to partner with us by sending His power to dwell within us through His Holy Spirit. We are commanded to be conduits of His healing for others.

Romans 8:11 says, "But if the Spirit of Him who raised Jesus from the dead dwells in you, He who raised Christ from the dead will also give life to your mortal bodies through His Spirit who dwells in you." Imagine the power at your disposal when you really accept that fact! God wants to use you to pray for people who are sick and oppressed by the devil. When someone is miraculously healed, it awakens a curiosity in others and stirs them to inquire about God. It opens the door for salvation in unbelievers and increases faith in believers. It ultimately inspires greater intimacy with God as people encounter His love and compassion in a very real and tangible way.

When the lame man was healed, people were able to see him the way God sees him. I am certain that it was "beautiful" to watch him walking, leaping, and praising God for his healing. John and Peter were also giving God all of the glory as they reminded the people that Jesus made this healing possible through His death, burial, and resurrection. This is a win-win-win situation! The lame man was set free, the disciples were encouraged, and God was glorified. Do you want to be made well? If you are willing, God is *always* ready.

Pause and Reflect
Prayerfully identify the areas of your spirit, soul, and body that need healing. Read Psalm 103 and Isaiah 58.

_____

_____

_____

_____

_____

_____

_____

_____

_____

_____

_____

_____

Raw and Real
There are far too many sick and afflicted Christians in the church.

Short and Sweet
Jesus, thank You for the price You paid for my healing. Heal my unbelief, Lord! Increase my faith and use me to set the captives free for Your glory. Amen.

Meditate and Memorize
"Now as the lame man who was healed held on to Peter and John, all the people ran together to them in the porch which is called Solomon's, greatly amazed."
—Acts 3:11

Believe and Receive
God still heals.

Listen and Learn

Ask God to heal you and use you.

_____

_____

_____

_____

_____

_____

_____

_____

_____

_____

_____

_____

_____

_____

_____

_____

_____

_____

_____

_____

_____

_____

_____

_____

_____

_____

_____

_____

_____

_____

_____

_____

Create and Relate
Use this space to connect with God through creativity.

ACTS 4
DAY FOUR

BOLDNESS

παῤῥησία

parrhēsia

par-rhay-see'-ah

outspokenness;
frankness, bluntness;
freedom in speaking;
assurance, cheerful courage;
free and fearless confidence

The most obvious shift in my life since I became a Christian is that of boldness. Once I tasted the goodness of God and received the baptism of the Holy Spirit, I started to speak with a confidence I had not previously known. I began to tell anyone and everyone about the power of the word of God and the true life I had found in Jesus Christ. This was not a natural thing for me. It came upon me quickly and forcefully when I made the decision to live wholeheartedly for the Lord.

Over the years, my boldness has increased. I never imagined that I would hold a microphone, share the gospel with the world, or write books that inspire people to study God's word. I have discovered so much freedom in obedience that I want to go wherever He sends me and say whatever He tells me. I can relate to Jeremiah when he said, "But His word was in my heart like a burning fire shut up in my bones; I was weary of holding it back, and I could not."[14] When there are rivers of living water rushing through your very being, you want the entire world to know about it! There is a shout inside of you that must find a way out. As you grow in your relationship with God and discover how good He truly is, you become desperate for people to know what you know.

We are not all called to preach from a pulpit, but we are all instructed by Jesus Himself to "Go into all the world and preach the gospel to every creature."[15] The word *preach* in that verse is the Greek word *kērussō*, and it means *to herald as a public crier, especially divine truth.* There is no mistaking what Jesus meant when He commissioned us to boldly proclaim the good news of the kingdom. You can express it verbally or creatively, through music or the arts. You can declare it in the marketplace, on the battlefield, at school, in sports, at church, at home, or wherever He leads you. He simply wants you to use the gifts He has given you to share His message with others. Are you doing that?

In Acts 4, we have front row seats at one of the best and boldest sermons ever preached. Verse 8 says, "Then Peter, filled with the Holy Spirit, said to them . . . ." Peter was an uneducated man, yet he stood before an intimidating Sanhedrin and spoke

[14] Jeremiah 20:9
[15] Mark 16:15

the truth with supernatural confidence. He delivered his message with authority and clarity. He not only defended the name of his Savior, but he did it in such a way that the gospel penetrated an unbelieving generation of leaders. None of this would have been possible had he not been filled with the Holy Spirit and empowered by the boldness of Almighty God.

I am nothing short of amazed at what happened next. Acts 4:13 says, "Now when they saw the boldness of Peter and John, and perceived that they were uneducated and untrained men, they marveled. And they realized that they had been with Jesus." Do you understand the implication of that statement? The time that Peter and John spent in close relationship with Jesus was evident to all. People *marveled* at the transformation that had occurred in their lives. If I live one hundred years, and the only thing anyone can say about me is, "She must have been with Jesus," I have accomplished what I came to do. Intimacy with Jesus should be the pursuit of our lives. It is the reason we exist. It is why God allowed Him to be crucified. The veil was torn so we can forever enter into the Holy of Holies. It is the greatest desire of God's heart. He wants all of His children to delight and rejoice in His beautiful presence.

Jesus said in John 14:6-7, "I am the way, the truth, and the life. No one comes to the Father except through Me. If you had known Me, you would have known My Father also; and from now on you know Him and have seen Him." Peter and John had physically been with Jesus on the earth for a time. Nothing else could compare to the intimacy they experienced with the Son of God in those few years. I imagine that they maximized every moment they had with Him, obediently following Him and willingly serving Him. I envision them asking questions and hanging on to every word as though their lives depended on it. They enjoyed meals with Him, watched as He performed miracles, and even had the glorious honor of attending Him in His greatest times of need. Intimacy is the by-product of nurturing a

> *Intimacy with Jesus should be the pursuit of our lives.*

relationship with another person. It was evident to even the most foreboding souls that these two men "had been with Jesus."

One of the most practical prayers in the Bible is the prayer for boldness that the family of believers prayed in Acts 4:24-30. Verses 29-30 say, ". . . grant to Your servants that with all boldness they may speak Your word, by stretching out Your hand to heal, and that signs and wonders may be done through the name of Your holy Servant Jesus." This is a simple prayer that anyone can pray. Verse 31 goes on to say, "And when they had prayed, the place where they were assembled together was shaken; and they were all filled with the Holy Spirit, and they spoke the word of God with boldness." This is clearly a prayer that God loves to answer!

I believe God wants to shake things up in His church again. There is a deficiency of boldness in the Body of Christ today. Millions of people around the world profess to be Christians, yet many lack the boldness that is required to be effective witnesses and followers of Christ. Acts 4:33 says, "And with great power the apostles gave witness to the resurrection of the Lord Jesus. And great grace was upon them all." God wants to reveal His power and His grace as He did in the first century. He wants to release a new fire and boldness to His servants. As you read the book of Acts, pay attention to the absolute confidence the believers possessed. Look again at what happened when they prayed for boldness. God's response literally shook the place as He filled them with His Spirit!

In Acts 4:20, Peter and John said, "For we cannot but speak the things which we have seen and heard." When you encounter God in supernatural ways, it will motivate you to tell others about His character and nature. When you understand what Jesus did for you, it will completely alter the way you live your life. When you experience His deep, abiding love, you will share it with those in need. When you invite His Holy Spirit to lead and guide you on a daily basis, opportunities will arise for you to deliver the good news to the lost. God will give you everything necessary to ensure that you are able to boldly do what He asks you to do.

Jesus was bold. He turned over tables in the temple in a fit of holy rage.[16] He cast a demon out of a man in the synagogue.[17] He became friends with sinners and outcasts. He interacted with the poor and uneducated people in society. He told the leaders exactly what was on His mind, and He always spoke the truth in love. It has been said that the truth hurts. It is not always fun to be the recipient of the truth, but it is sometimes even more difficult to be the messenger. Apart from God's gift of boldness, it is nearly impossible to deliver His truth to an unbelieving and rebellious world.

Have you ever found yourself in a situation where the Holy Spirit prompted you to be bold about a particular issue that grieved His heart? How did you handle it? Did you respond obediently by declaring His truth or did you ignore His prompting and allow darkness to prevail? Boldness enables you to do the hard thing. Yes, it can be risky. Yes, it can be challenging. Yes, it can even cause you to lose friends at times, but we need to learn to fear God more than we fear man. Obedience opens doors for greater encounters with God. You cannot expect miracles, signs, and wonders to mark your life if you do not stand for truth in the little things.

Allow me to clarify that boldness does not give anyone permission to display abusive, critical, condemning, or degrading behavior. It does, however, mean that you seize every opportunity you are given by the Lord to make His truth known—and to do so with love. Remember that Jesus *is* the truth, and He is also love.

Proverbs 28:1 says, "The wicked flee when no one pursues, but the righteous are bold as a lion." You have been made righteous through the blood of the Lamb. Remember that this gentle, spotless Lamb of God is also known as the roaring Lion of Judah. You will need boldness through His Holy Spirit to reveal Him to a lost and dying generation. 2 Timothy 1:7 says,

> *Obedience opens doors for greater encounters with God.*

---

16   Matthew 21:12-13
17   Luke 4:33-35

"For God has not given us a spirit of fear, but of power and of love and of a sound mind." Shake off timidity and renew your mind to the empowering word of God. Incorporate the Acts 4 prayer into your daily life until you are certain that it has been answered . . . then ask for more!

Pause and Reflect

How will an increase in boldness impact the way you share your faith with others?

_____

_____

_____

_____

_____

_____

_____

_____

_____

_____

_____

_____

Raw and Real

The preacher is not the only one who is called to boldly proclaim the gospel.

Short and Sweet

Lord, I need You. Apart from You I can do nothing. Fill me with boldness and help me be obedient in the little things. Use me to confidently declare the good news to all creation. Amen.

Meditate and Memorize

". . . grant to Your servants that with all boldness they may speak Your word, by stretching out Your hand to heal, and that signs and wonders may be done through the name of Your holy Servant Jesus."

—Acts 4:29-30

Believe and Receive

I am bold as a lion.

Listen and Learn

Write your own prayer for boldness.

_____

_____

_____

_____

_____

_____

_____

_____

_____

_____

_____

_____

_____

_____

_____

_____

_____

_____

_____

_____

_____

_____

_____

_____

_____

_____

_____

_____

_____

_____

Create and Relate
Use this space to connect with God through creativity.

TRUTH

ἀλήθεια

alētheia

al-ay'-thi-a

not concealing;
without falsehood and deceit;
free from pretense and simulation

Do you believe that the word of God is absolute truth? Once you settle this issue in your heart, divine beauty and love will begin to flood your life with enduring certitude. There are many debates and discrepancies, even among Christians, regarding the inerrancy of the word of God. I can assure you that there will never be an answer to every question that is posed concerning the validity of God's word. It is accepted *by faith*, and a supernatural discernment is awakened within one's soul confirming that the words in the Bible are God-breathed. Barring time and space, we could study the original manuscripts and enjoy the fruit of God's truth together. I cannot elaborate historically, scientifically, theoretically, or theologically here. I can, however, share my personal experience with you and hope that it provokes a greater hunger in your life for truth.

I began my journey into the heart of God when I was thirty-one years old. I spent my formative years in Catholic church and school, but I never picked up a Bible and read it with a genuine desire to *know* God. I lived the majority of my life lying to myself and to others about who I was and what I was doing. I was trying to be someone that I was not for the sole purpose of pleasing people. I wanted to believe that I had value and worth so I fabricated a life that convinced absolutely no one that I was satisfied and successful. I searched for true peace and joy in people, places, and things, but I came up empty every time. I finally hit rock bottom in 2005 and realized that there had to be more to life than what I was experiencing. As you may know, when you are at rock bottom, there is only one place to look . . . UP! So I prayed. I confessed my weaknesses and inadequacies to a God I had never known. I repented of my sins, and I cried out for Him to reveal the *truth* about Himself and change my life forever. Then I picked up my Bible.

I remember reading the Bible previously and wondering how anyone could enjoy such a boring, tedious book. My heart had been so hardened by sin that it was seemingly impenetrable by the life-giving words on those pages. It was not until I acknowledged my desperation and *need* for God that the Bible began to pierce my soul. Once my heart and mind were opened to the *reality* of a loving Creator and the *possibility* of

His truth affecting my life, I was finally able to *receive* what He wanted to give me. Only then did I begin to understand what millions of others have understood for centuries. *The word of God is truth.* It is absolute. It is life. It is healing and wholeness. It is food for the spirit, soul, and body. It is an instruction manual and love letter all at the same time. It is the very tool God would use to introduce Himself to me in ways I had never dreamt were possible.

I share this with you because I want you to know that it was the Breath of God (Holy Spirit) on the Word of God (Jesus) that set me on a fiery path to discover who I am and why I am here. I still give my life to God in a new way every day as I read His word. It helps me remember that He loves me like no one else can. I have a grateful heart as I consider that He made a way for me to spend eternity in His presence. The Bible teaches about salvation, consecration, and sanctification. It gives direction regarding how to love God, love myself, and love others. It confirms my purpose and ignites my passion. It reveals who Jesus is and what He did for me. The word of God comforts and convicts me. It encourages, inspires, and heals me. Hebrews 4:12 says, "For the word of God is living and powerful, and sharper than any two-edged sword, piercing even to the division of soul and spirit, and of joints and marrow, and is a discerner of the thoughts and intents of the heart." God's word moves me in miraculous ways, revealing wrong attitudes and impure motives of which I may otherwise be unaware. His divine truth continues to lead and guide me as I follow Him by faith and live for His glory.

It was the *truth* that set me on a path to freedom in 2005. I continually realize that I have been sabotaged by lies and deception since the moment I entered this world. John 8:44 says that Satan ". . . does not stand in the truth, because there is no truth in him. When he speaks a lie, he speaks from his own resources, for he is a liar and the father of it." In stark contrast, Numbers 23:19 says, "God is not a man, that He should lie." *Truth is who God is.* Jesus is the embodiment of that truth, and His word is the conduit of everything pure, holy, and right. I challenge you to contemplate whose character you exhibit on a daily basis as we take a look at truth versus lies in the fifth chapter of Acts.

God is very serious about the benefits of truth and the consequences of lies. Romans 6:23 tells us, "For the wages of sin is death, but the gift of God is eternal life in Christ Jesus our Lord." Lying is a sin, and there is a price to pay for that sin. In Acts 5:1-11, we witness the severity of this sin as Ananias and Sapphira lied about withholding part of the proceeds from a sale they made. In Acts 5:3-4, Peter asked, "Ananias, why has Satan filled your heart to lie to the Holy Spirit . . . Why have you conceived this thing in your heart? You have not lied to men but to God." Immediate death was God's response to the lies told by this couple. I ponder in amazement at this New Testament act of justice. God was establishing and implementing something new in the church of Acts. I believe He wanted to make His commitment to truth very clear to everyone at the beginning. His intention was to create a pure and holy family of believers who would set an example for the world to follow. Lying and deception could have no place in this new way of life.

> *Truth is who God is.*

Some would say that death was not necessary. Perhaps a reprimanding or a disciplinary action of some sort would have been a better response to the lies told by Ananias and Sapphira. After all, Jesus had just died for this, right? What happened to grace and mercy? I believe God wanted to make a statement in the early church that would impact the heart of every believer thereafter. Jesus IS the truth![18] For someone to identify with Him as a Christian means that he or she agrees to conform to His very nature and identity. He is the antithesis to darkness and sin. His death, burial, and resurrection serve as a beacon of hope to an ever-seeking world. To *knowingly* partake in anything contrary to the truth is a slap in His face. For this reason, the Author of all that is pure and holy boldly revealed Himself through the unexpected deaths of Ananias

---

[18] John 14:6

and Sapphira. It was as if He was saying, *"STOP! This is not who I am!"*

1 John 1:5-7 says, ". . . God is light and in Him is no darkness at all. If we say that we have fellowship with Him, and walk in darkness, we lie and do not practice the truth. But if we walk in the light as He is in the light, we have fellowship with one another, and the blood of Jesus Christ His Son cleanses us from all sin."

The comparison and contrast between truth and deception in this particular chapter is not to be overlooked. Immediately after Ananias and Sapphira were struck dead for their disobedience, God revealed what truth in action in the lives of believers really looks like. The apostles operated in signs and wonders, leading multitudes to salvation, because they lived radical lives of transparency and truth. Transparency is not always easy, but it is necessary in order to be honest with yourself and others. Remember that God already knows the truth about every area of your life. One of your responsibilities as a Christian is to expose the darkness in and around you. The enemy of your soul will be evicted as you *reveal* what he wants to keep hidden in the dark. Jesus is the light of the world.[19] Darkness cannot stand in His presence or in the presence of Spirit-filled believers who submit to truth in their lives. The apostles believed the truth, spoke the truth, lived the truth, and represented the One who *is* absolute truth. Throughout history, people have been set free from sickness and bondage as they received and believed the truth of God's word.

Jesus said, "If you abide in My word, you are My disciples indeed. And you shall know the truth, and the truth shall make you free."[20] God does not expect perfection, but He does look favorably upon a pure heart. Unfortunately, Ananias and Sapphira had impurity in their hearts related to money and possessions. They not only lied to men and to God, but they also lied to themselves. They wanted others to believe they had given all they had. They were ultimately trapped in a lie of appearances. They were wrapped up in *religion* and completely

---

[19] John 8:12
[20] John 8:31-32

blind to being in right *relationship* with God. They were also prideful, assuming at some point that they could outwit their Creator.

Lying has become commonplace in society today. Leaders of nations, corporations, and churches have fallen prey to blatant lies and deception. Lies, cheating and scandals abound in every realm of society. People we looked "up" to have been exposed for their lack of morality and ethics. Families are being ripped apart daily because of lies. No one is exempt. As Christians, we are called to speak the truth, to teach and preach the truth, to live the truth, and to love the truth. Think about the words you speak. Are they truthful? Are you honoring God by living an honest life? Are you a man or woman of your word? When you say something, can it be trusted? When you speak, do people believe you or do they question your integrity?

Revelation 21:8 says, "But the cowardly, unbelieving, abominable, murderers, sexually immoral, sorcerers, idolaters, and all liars shall have their part in the lake which burns with fire and brimstone, which is the second death." Holy fear is a good thing. We serve a holy God who wants His truth, Jesus, revealed to all of mankind. He wants the captives to be released from the grip of the enemy, who is the father of all lies. Even in Christian circles, truth can be exaggerated and embellished in such a way that it no longer bears any resemblance to the actual truth.

> *Are you honoring God by living an honest life?*

Ephesians 4:25 says, "Therefore, putting away lying, 'Let each one of you speak truth with his neighbor,' for we are members of one another." Make a decision to speak with the boldness of heaven and release truth into the atmosphere around you at all times. Consider Matthew 5:14-16: "You are the light of the world. A city that is set on a hill cannot be hidden. Nor do they light a lamp and put it under a basket, but on a lampstand, and it gives light to all who are in the house. Let your light so shine before men, that they may see your good works and glorify your Father in heaven." Let your light shine today, beloved, in truth and love! It is one of the most powerful ways to display the character and nature of Christ.

Pause and Reflect

Pinpoint the areas of your life where you have been dishonest with yourself, with others, or with God. How will the knowledge of the truth change the way you live?

_____

_____

_____

_____

_____

_____

_____

_____

_____

_____

_____

_____

Raw and Real

Many people sitting in the pews are living lives of deception and dishonesty.

Short and Sweet

Father of all that is right and good, forgive me for the times that my speech and life have been less than truthful. Renew my mind to Your holy word. Amen.

Meditate and Memorize

"Why have you conceived this thing in your heart? You have not lied to men but to God."
—Acts 5:4

Believe and Receive

I will speak the truth at all times.

Listen and Learn
Confess your sins and ask for forgiveness.

_____

_____

_____

_____

_____

_____

_____

_____

_____

_____

_____

_____

_____

_____

_____

_____

_____

_____

_____

_____

_____

_____

_____

_____

_____

_____

_____

_____

_____

_____

_____

_____

_____

_____

_____

Create and Relate
Use this space to connect with God through creativity.

ACTS 6
DAY SIX

FAITH

πίστις

pistis

pis'-tis

assurance, fidelity;
conviction of the truth of anything;
belief with the idea of trust or confidence

The theme of faith is scattered throughout the word of God. There is an entire chapter in the book of Hebrews dedicated to this subject that has confounded mankind for thousands of years. The topic of faith has caused rifts between friends, families, and nations. It has wreaked havoc on the world's political systems and has been a catalyst for many wars. This little five-letter word encompasses a field of thought that has produced countless volumes of books and endless resources in every culture around the globe. Faith is a dynamic conversation starter and quite possibly an equally as dynamic conversation ender. It is an innate component of the human nature to have faith in something or someone. Yes, even if you do not believe in God, you are placing your faith in the fact that He does not exist. Everyone possesses faith.

Faith is a fascinating concept. By definition, it is a strongly held theory or belief in a particular system of thought, devotion, or worship. It implies complete confidence and trust in something or someone. *Faith in Jesus Christ* is the foundation of Christianity, upon which the remainder of our lives is built. Although denominational teachings may vary, the core fundamentals of our faith stand united. So what exactly are these basic tenets of the Christian faith and how do we practically apply them to our lives?

> *Everyone possesses faith.*

There are essentially five core doctrines an individual should adhere to as a Bible-believing Christian: The Inspiration and Inerrancy of Scripture; The Virgin Birth; The Incarnation and Deity of Jesus Christ; The Blood Atonement; and The Bodily Resurrection. Let us take a closer look at each of these elements as they concern the faith of a Christ-centered, Spirit-baptized believer.

The first doctrine is The Inerrancy of Scripture. 2 Timothy 3:16-17 says, "All Scripture is given by inspiration of God, and is profitable for doctrine, for reproof, for correction, for instruction in righteousness, that the man of God may be complete, thoroughly equipped for every good work." Our faith is in the Holy Bible as the inspired word of God, completely infallible and sufficient for all Christian life. By "inspired" we mean that the Holy Spirit breathed His supernatural influence upon the writers of the Bible. One of the greatest attacks on the Christian faith today is regarding the authority and accuracy of Scripture. Some people may say, "No, Jesus is the issue—not the Bible," but I argue that Jesus *as He is presented in the Bible* is the issue. Without faith in the Bible as the holy, trustworthy truth, we cannot rightly believe any of the other fundamental doctrines. A strong faith declares, "If the Bible says it, that settles it!" If you do not believe the Bible, Jesus cannot become real to you. Slight variations in meanings of words occur through translation, but the authenticity and reliability of the word of God stands proven for nearly two thousand years. What is the foundation of your faith, really, if it is not the word of God?

The second doctrine is The Virgin Birth. Luke 1:35 says, "And the angel answered and said to her, 'The Holy Spirit will come upon you, and the power of the Highest will overshadow you; therefore, also, that Holy One who is to be born will be called the Son of God.'" The virgin birth of Jesus Christ is unparalleled in all of human history. Isaiah prophesied this miraculous event seven hundred years before it occurred: "Therefore the Lord Himself will give you a sign: Behold, the virgin shall conceive and bear a Son, and shall call His name Immanuel."[21] It was by the virgin birth that God became man. This leads us to the third doctrine of the Christian faith—Incarnation.

The third core truth of Christianity involves the Deity of our Lord Jesus Christ. John 1:1-2 tells us, "In the beginning was the Word, and the Word was with God, and the Word was God. He was in the beginning with God." Then John 1:14 says, "And the Word became flesh and dwelt among us, and we beheld His glory, the glory as of the only begotten of the Father, full of grace and truth." God manifested Himself in the bodily form of Jesus Christ to dwell among men. This doctrine of the faith emphatically states that Jesus is 100% God and 100% man. This is well established in the New Testament (Matthew 14:33; Matthew 28:18; Mark 2:5-11; John 1:1; John 8:51-58; John

---

[21]   Isaiah 7:14

17:5; John 20:28; Colossians 1:16-17; Hebrews 1:1-4; Hebrews 1:8.)

The fourth doctrine is that of The Blood Atonement. As stated in the Old Testament, "And according to the law almost all things are purified with blood, and without shedding of blood there is no remission."[22] In Matthew 26:28, Jesus said, "For this is My blood of the new covenant, which is shed for many for the remission of sins." Jesus died a substitutionary death on a cross for the forgiveness of our sins. God Himself poured out His blood for mankind. Philippians 2:8 says, "And being found in appearance as a man, He humbled Himself and became obedient to the point of death, even the death of the cross." He came to die. His blood set us free.

The fifth and final doctrine is that of The Bodily Resurrection. In John 11:25-26, Jesus said, "I am the resurrection and the life. He who believes in Me, though he may die, he shall live. And whoever lives and believes in Me shall never die." Jesus died a brutal death and was buried. Three days later, He rose from the dead. His resurrected body was witnessed by many, including: the women returning from the grave (Matthew 28:5-10); the two men on the road to Emmaus (Luke 24); Mary Magdalene, the apostles, and many other disciples (Luke 24; John 20; Acts 1). In his letter to the Corinthians, the Apostle Paul recounts, "For I delivered to you first of all that which I also received: that Christ died for our sins according to the Scriptures, and that He was buried, and that He rose again the third day according to the Scriptures, and that He was seen by Cephas, then by the twelve. After that He was seen by over five hundred brethren at once, of whom the greater part remain to the present, but some have fallen asleep. After that He was seen by James, then by all the apostles. Then last of all He was seen by me also, as by one born out of due time." [23] After His resurrection, Jesus ascended into heaven and sent His Spirit to dwell within the bodies of believers. He will return again someday to rule and reign on earth.

---

[22]   Hebrews 9:22

[23]   1 Corinthians 15:3-8

These five tenets of Christianity keep us grounded in our belief system. Faith takes root. It is not something shallow and fading. It requires a sound understanding of *why* you believe *what* you believe. It does not change like the tide or the wind, nor does it shift like sand. It becomes a part of your very being. Your faith forms your identity. It determines the course of your life. It will lead and guide you in your relationships, career, and recreational activities. Renouncing "faith" is not simply rejecting a particular religious affiliation. It is denying the fact that every one of us has placed a belief in something or someone. In that denial, there is a conscious or subconscious decision to choose *not* to serve the one true living God. How do I know there is only One and that He is alive and true? I know by faith.

> *Your faith forms your identity.*

Acts 6 is a short chapter infused with a powerful message about faith. The disciples were making some important decisions as they continued to spread the gospel. Seven wise and faith-filled men were chosen to preside over the business of serving the Hellenistic widows. Among these men was Stephen, whom the Bible specifically refers to as "full of faith and the Holy Spirit." [24] As we will discover in Acts 7, Stephen became the first known Christian martyr. He was persecuted and killed for what he believed in. He was stoned to death for his *faith* in Jesus Christ as Messiah. This man, Stephen, never renounced his beliefs, even unto the brutal ending of his life.

Acts 6:8 says, "And Stephen, full of faith and power, did great wonders and signs among the people." I want to be certain that this correlation is not missed. *It is impossible to do great wonders and signs for the glory of God apart from being filled with faith and the power of the Holy Spirit.* It is also important to note that faith and power are not mutually exclusive. The Greek word for power in that verse is *dunamis*, and it refers to miraculous, mighty, wonderful works. Faith and power work together. We must activate our Christian faith and allow God's supernatural power to flow in and through

---

[24]   Acts 6:5

us. Only then will unbelievers see the fruit of the faith we possess.

It is an inborn desire of every human to have faith in something or someone. This leads to an unfortunate tendency to place too much confidence and trust in people, organizations, government, politics, financial systems, self, or even inanimate objects. This often results in idolatry and ultimately sin. We must be certain that our faith is in God alone, that it is based on the fundamentals of Christianity, and that it is *alive* and *active*. James 2:17 says, "Thus also faith by itself, if it does not have works, is dead."

According to Hebrews 11:1, "Now faith is the substance of things hoped for, the evidence of things not seen." 2 Corinthians 5:7 says, "For we walk by faith, not by sight." As Christians, we do not rely on our natural eyesight to confirm that Jesus is the Son of God, that He died, was buried, and rose again, and that He sent His Holy Spirit to dwell within us. We believe it and accept it *by faith*. Hebrews 11:6 reminds us, "But without faith it is impossible to please Him, for he who comes to God must believe that He is, and that He is a rewarder of those who diligently seek Him." Faith is the very foundation upon which Christianity is built. People live by it and die for it every day around the world. Are you full of faith and power as Stephen and the disciples in Acts were? All you have to do is believe.

Pause and Reflect
In what or whom do you place your faith? If someone asked you to explain your faith, could you do it?

_____

_____

_____

_____

_____

_____

_____

_____

_____

_____

_____

_____

_____

_____

Raw and Real
Wonders and signs are rare today because of rampant unbelief among Christians.

Short and Sweet
Lord, I believe! Increase my faith and teach me how to activate it for Your glory. Help me place complete confidence and trust in You all the days of my life. Amen.

Meditate and Memorize
"And Stephen, full of faith and power, did great wonders and signs among the people."
—Acts 6:8

Believe and Receive
I am full of faith and the Holy Spirit.

Listen and Learn
Explore your faith.

_____

_____

_____

_____

_____

_____

_____

_____

_____

_____

_____

_____

_____

_____

_____

_____

_____

_____

_____

_____

_____

_____

_____

_____

_____

_____

_____

_____

_____

_____

_____

_____

_____

_____

Create and Relate

Use this space to connect with God through creativity.

ACTS 7
DAY SEVEN

WITNESS

μαρτύριον

marturion

mar-too'-ree-on

testimony;
something evidential;
generally evidence given;
specifically the Decalogue
(Ten Commandments) in the
sacred Tabernacle

In Acts 1:8 Jesus said, "But you shall receive power when the Holy Spirit has come upon you; and you shall be witnesses to Me in Jerusalem, and in all Judea and Samaria, and to the end of the earth." The Greek word for *witnesses* in that verse is *martus*, from which the English word *martyr* is derived. It refers to those who have proven the authenticity of their faith in Christ by enduring a violent death. A *witness*, according to this definition, is someone who embodies the evidential and testimonial aspect of Christianity, even unto death. That is pretty radical, if you ask me. It makes me wonder if we truly understand this commission we have been given by Christ.

Witness is also a legal and judicial term. It conjures up images of someone giving a sworn testimony to a court of law. In that regard, a witness typically has first-hand knowledge of an event pertaining to a crime or accident. In the book of Acts, people were martyred for their faith in Christ, and they also testified of His death, burial, and resurrection. Being a witness in the first century looked very different than it does in many parts of the world today. What does it really mean to be a witness for Christ? Does it mean that you don your favorite "Jesus is my homeboy" t-shirt and hit the streets on a Friday night to share the gospel or does it mean that you meet in an underground church in a third-world country and pray that you make it out alive? Witness is not only something you *do*, it is *who you are*. The way you speak, think, and act on a daily basis is a testimony to others of the light and love of Christ within you.

I find it interesting that Jesus promised His disciples *power* first in Acts 1:8 before He identified them as His witnesses. He was essentially telling them that they had to be properly equipped before they could do the work He had called them to do. He knew that they would not be effective apart from the power and anointing of the Holy Spirit. A weak and powerless Christian is not capable of delivering the kind of speech Stephen delivered in Acts 7. Acts 6:8 reminds us, "And Stephen, full of faith and power, did great wonders and signs among the people." This is the same miracle-working ability that Jesus referred to in Acts 1:8. We need His *power* to witness.

As the first known martyr and one of the greatest witnesses in the book of Acts, Stephen set a standard for all who would follow him. His death in Acts 7 should provoke the reader to ask some tough questions. Do I love Jesus that much? Am I really willing to give my life for this faith? Can I truly defend something that my

> *Witness is not only something you do, it is who you are.*

physical eye has not seen? Will my testimony be authentic enough to stir hearts and change lives, as Stephen's was?

Stephen was a brave man, a man of courage and faith. In his final moments, he declared the truth about who God is to an unbelieving Jewish council. He shared a testimony of the reality and goodness of God throughout history, beginning with the patriarchs and closing with a reference to the Holy Spirit. Toward the end of his address, Stephen made an interesting reference to "the tabernacle of witness." I want to elaborate on the word *witness* in this context and hopefully inspire you to see things as Stephen saw them. Without a better understanding of the importance of this phrase, we cannot fully appreciate why the Jews were so convicted and enraged by Stephen's words.

The tabernacle of witness is first mentioned in Exodus 25. God instructed Moses in Exodus 25:8-9, "And let them make Me a sanctuary, that I may dwell among them. According to all that I show you, that is, the pattern of the tabernacle and the pattern of all its furnishings, just so you shall make it." The word *sanctuary* in verse 8 is closely related to words that translate as consecrate, sanctify, holy, and holiness. The word *tabernacle* in verse 9 refers to a residence or dwelling place. This tabernacle would be a holy habitation for a holy God. It would be a place of consecration, sanctification, and sacrifice. It would be the meeting ground upon which God and man would interact.

Beyond the veil in this tabernacle was a small piece of furniture known as the ark of the covenant, also called the ark of the *testimony*. Above the ark was the mercy seat, or throne of God, where the fiery presence of the Lord rested. Moses and the high priest were the only people allowed to enter this most holy place. Exodus 25:21-22 says, "You shall put the mercy seat on top of the ark, and in the ark you shall put the Testimony that I will give you. And there I will meet with you, and I will speak with you from above the mercy seat, from between the two cherubim which are on the ark of the Testimony, about everything which I will give you in commandment to the children of Israel." The Hebrew word translated as *testimony* in those verses is *edut*. It literally means *witness*. What exactly is the Testimony, and why did God command Moses to place it in the ark of the covenant?

The Testimony in that passage of Scripture refers to the Ten Commandments. This was the moral code God gave Moses, written on stone, and also known as the tablets of the Law. They represented the word of God—a testimony of Jesus Christ, the Word made flesh. They prophetically pointed to Jesus as the promised Messiah of the Jewish people. They were also a constant reminder and witness of His presence, provoking and convicting them to obey His laws. As the Israelites wandered through the wilderness, God was with them. They were counseled, convicted, refreshed, and sustained by His presence in this tabernacle of witness.

Today, we no longer rely on words written on cold stone tablets to remind us that God's presence is among us. Instead, we have the glorious honor of abiding with the Word of God daily through His Spirit. 1 Corinthians 6:19-20 says, "Or do you not know that your body is the temple of the Holy Spirit who is in you, whom you have from God, and you are not your own? For you were bought at a price; therefore glorify God in your body and in your spirit, which are God's." The ultimate price was paid for our sins when the spotless Lamb of God shed His blood for those He loves. The witness of God's glory and presence now resides within the temple of every believer's mortal body.

In Acts 7:48, Stephen said, "However, the Most High does not dwell in temples made with hands . . . ." 2 Corinthians 3:3 confirms this, ". . . clearly you are an epistle of Christ, ministered by us, written not with ink but by the Spirit of the living God, not on tablets of stone but on tablets of flesh, that is, of the heart." When you know the Lord Jesus as Savior, your heart becomes His throne. The Word of God abides within you. You *become* God's holy dwelling place. When His Spirit fills you, He empowers you to *be* His *tabernacle of witness.* You are a living, breathing, tangible testimony of His reality. Your life is an expression of His goodness, power, love, and mercy. He is always near, as a faithful witness to the world of who He really is.

Jesus made a way for you to be in the presence of God once again. You no longer have to stand outside the camp, as the Israelites did, while the high priest enters the holy place on your behalf. The burning fire and glory of the Lord abide within you! That fact alone should radically alter the way you live your life. Wherever you go, the presence of the Lord goes also. He sees everything you do. He hears everything you say. Is your life a reflection of the holy God who lives within you?

Stephen mentioned the tabernacle of witness just before he rebuked the devout Jews in Acts 7:51: "You stiff-necked and uncircumcised in heart and ears! You always resist the Holy Spirit; as your fathers did, so do you." The Jews did not acknowledge the Holy Spirit. They accepted the fact that the presence of God rested on a wooden box overlaid with gold in a tent in the wilderness, but they did not believe that He could supernaturally dwell within them through His Spirit. They rejected Christ, and they refused His Spirit.

> *You are a living, breathing, tangible testimony of His reality.*

Stephen, empowered by the Holy Spirit, delivered a testimony graced with authority and truth. It radically stirred the enemy's camp and provoked the unbelieving Jews to murder. Acts 7:54-60 says, "When they heard these things they were cut to the heart, and they gnashed at him with their teeth . . . And they stoned Stephen as he was calling on God and saying, 'Lord Jesus, receive my spirit.' Then he knelt down and cried out with a loud voice, 'Lord, do not charge them with this sin.' And when he had said this, he fell asleep."

Stephen's boldness and courage witnessed to all who heard his final words. His forgiveness was a testimony of the love of God in action. He knew that his faith in Christ could lead to his death, and he reasoned that it was worth it. Stephen proudly proclaimed the truth and let his beautiful light shine until the moment he took his last breath.

One of the greatest honors Christians have been given is to *become* a tabernacle of witness, as Stephen did, and carry God's presence to the ends of the earth. Are you living as a holy habitation who exemplifies what it means to be a witness in this hour of history? Prayerfully consider the definition of witness today and allow the Holy Spirit to use you to reveal Christ to others.

Pause and Reflect

How is your life a testimony of God's power and purity? Do you treat your body as though it is the dwelling place of the *Holy Spirit*?

_____

_____

_____

_____

_____

_____

_____

_____

_____

_____

Raw and Real

It is impossible to be a witness for Christ apart from the indwelling power of the Holy Spirit.

Short and Sweet

Holy Spirit, empower me to be a bold witness for You, remembering always that my body is Your holy dwelling place. Show me Your glory and use me to testify of Your goodness. Amen.

Meditate and Memorize

"Our fathers had the tabernacle of witness in the wilderness, as He appointed, instructing Moses to make it according to the pattern that he had seen . . . ."
—Acts 7:44

Believe and Receive

My body is a temple.

Listen and Learn

Contemplate what it means to be a witness.

_____

_____

_____

_____

_____

_____

_____

_____

_____

_____

_____

_____

_____

_____

_____

_____

_____

_____

_____

_____

_____

_____

_____

_____

_____

_____

_____

_____

_____

_____

_____

_____

_____

Create and Relate
Use this space to connect with God through creativity.

ACTS 8
DAY EIGHT

PREACH

εὐαγγελίζω

euaggelizō

yoo-ang-ghel-id'-zo

evangelize;
to announce good news;
to declare or bring glad tidings

In the final chapter of Mark's gospel, the resurrected Jesus appeared to the eleven disciples. First, He rebuked their unbelief and hardness of heart. Then He gave them a great commission. He commanded them to "Go into all the world and preach the gospel to every creature."[25] Have you ever considered what Jesus meant by that? He spoke something so simple yet so profound that it has impacted generations of Christians for nearly two thousand years. What was it about that statement to "go" and "preach" that was so important? Why did He choose to leave them with that particular instruction before He ascended to heaven?

The eighth chapter of Acts makes over half a dozen references to preaching in a mere forty verses. It is a significant chapter concerning the directive of Jesus to preach the gospel. It establishes a pattern and guideline for all believers everywhere to follow. It reveals the certainty that God's word is absolute truth. This chapter is an excellent reminder that His promises are intended for *all* who believe. It teaches us that faith and obedience produce supernatural fruit. It encourages us that we, too, are called to experience God's great power as we share the gospel with others.

Unfortunately, too many people believe that preaching is only for the man or woman behind the pulpit. Christian, the *world* is your pulpit. Hear my heart on this: I do not have a problem with someone standing in front of a congregation delivering the word, empowering the people, and shepherding the flock. I believe this is the will of God. However, we must not allow the platform to get in the way of the Presence. When that happens, it becomes difficult to walk in true power and authority.

We cannot become bound to our buildings if we want to see God move. We are each called to go wherever He tells us to go and say whatever He tells us to say. The men and women in the book of Acts witnessed miraculous and supernatural events on a regular basis. They *believed* what Jesus said and they *acted* on it out of sincere love for Him and genuine compassion for others. They preached because He told them to, but they also

[25] Mark 16:15

preached because they had something they wanted people to know. They knew that true life could only be found in Christ, and they recognized that the answer to every problem was in His name. This was something they could not help but tell the world about!

What exactly does it look like to "preach" today? Is it the televangelist encouraging 50,000 people in a basketball arena? What about the missionary living in the dirt with orphans in a third world country? Could it be the father who leads his son to Christ as he tucks him into bed? Perhaps it is the CEO who is not afraid to use the name of Jesus in his board meetings. Maybe it is the soldier who shares the gospel with a dying comrade on the battlefield or the nurse who says a prayer for a sick patient. Wherever you are, whatever you are doing, you have an opportunity to preach.

> *We must not allow the platform to get in the way of the Presence.*

Thankfully, Acts 8 teaches us *how* to preach, *what* to preach, and to *whom* we should preach. There are a total of seven specific references to preaching in this brief chapter. Each one helps us understand what it is that we are supposed to do as individuals, and as a corporate body of believers, who are called to preach. Meditate on the following italicized phrases as you read and allow the Holy Spirit to make them personal.

Acts 8:4 tells us that the scattered *believers went everywhere preaching the word*. Acts 8:5 says that Philip *preached Christ to the multitudes* in Samaria. Verse 8:12 goes on to say that Philip *preached the things concerning the kingdom of God and the name of Jesus Christ*. In Acts 8:25, Peter and John *testified and preached the word of the Lord*. They also *preached the gospel in many villages*. Philip *opened his mouth* in verse 35 and *preached Jesus* to the Ethiopian eunuch. Finally, in verse 40, Philip *preached in all the cities he passed through* on his way to Caesarea.

Wow! There is a plethora of information in those few verses. *Who* preached? The disciples did. *Where* did they preach? Anywhere the Lord would lead them. *To whom* did they preach? To everyone—individuals and entire cities! *What* did they preach? They preached Jesus. They preached the word of God and the things concerning the kingdom of God. They preached the gospel. *How* did they preach? They opened their mouths.

Three different Greek words are translated as *preached* or *preaching* in this chapter. The most often used verb is *euaggelizō*.[26] The English word *evangelize* is derived from this word. It refers to announcing or declaring good news. Verse 5 uses the word *kērussō*, which implies the public proclamation of the gospel. Then verse 25 uses a third word, *laleō*. By definition, it is the actual act of speaking, including the emission of sounds from the mouth and the use of the tongue to articulate words. All of these references to preaching involve the verbal delivery of the gospel.

St. Francis of Assissi once said, "Preach the gospel at all times. If necessary, use words." Your actions, character, and integrity often speak louder than your words. We have all encountered people (or possibly even been one of them) who offer an awful lot of lip service but do not live a lifestyle that backs it up. This is not God's way. He is looking for believers who will exemplify Christ in word *and* deed.[27] The preachers in Acts 8 not only *talked* about the word of God, but they *embodied* it. In other words, they practiced what they preached. God's word *will* accomplish what it has been sent to accomplish, but we must each do our part to ensure that everyone has an opportunity to receive it. That requires opening our mouths to release it and living our lives in obedience to it.

Acts 8 reveals the undeniable fact that preaching involves uttering words and proclaiming truth. You do not have to be educated or articulate, nor do you need anyone's permission. Jesus has already given you permission in Mark 16:15. He has given you everything you need to preach with power and authority. Regardless of age, sex, race, or denomination, if you

---

[26]   Acts 8:4, 12, 35, 40
[27]   Colossians 3:17

are a follower of Christ, you have a personal testimony of how Jesus has impacted your life. His love covers a multitude of sins, and His Spirit empowers you to live a life of purpose. [28] *You have the greatest weapon in the history of arsenals at your disposal in the form of the Holy Bible.* The only thing preventing you from preaching is your own attitude about it and possibly a fear of man.

Are you called to preach? Absolutely. What that looks like is up to you and God, based on His purpose for your life. I do not know exactly where you will go or to whom you will preach, but I do know that you *will* preach. It is the greatest commission Jesus has given you. The believers who have gone before you in the book of Acts have set the bar pretty high. Let them inspire you to take your relationship with Him to a new level as you pick up where they left off.

> *"Go into all the world and preach the gospel to every creature."*
>
> *Mark 16:15*

You may not be a full-time traveling missionary like the Apostle Paul or a worldwide crusading evangelist like the Reverend Billy Graham, but if you call yourself a Christian, you *will* preach. Do not despise it. Embrace it. One of the greatest blessings in life is to experience the pleasure of sharing the gospel with someone and watching a life take on new meaning after encountering Jesus.

Jesus was a preacher. We cannot follow Him apart from doing what He did and saying what He said. Mark 16:20 says, "And they went out and preached everywhere, the Lord working with them and confirming the word through the accompanying signs." The Spirit of the Lord was *with* them as they did His work. The believers in Acts 8 had the glorious opportunity to witness the presence and power of God as they obeyed His voice. Multitudes were saved and baptized, demons were cast out, the lame were healed, miracles were performed, and people received the Holy Spirit. Acts 8:8 says, "And there was great joy in that city."

---

[28] 1 Peter 4:8, Proverbs 10:12

How could there not be?! This is the fruit of preaching the gospel God's way. Open your mouth and let Him speak through you today as you share His word with someone in need. Go! Preach!

Pause and Reflect

Has your life reflected the command of Jesus in Mark 16:15 to "preach the gospel?" If not, why not? What have you learned from the believers in Acts about preaching?

_____

_____

_____

_____

_____

_____

_____

_____

_____

_____

_____

_____

Raw and Real

Preaching is not intended to establish man's kingdom, rather to reveal the truth about God's.

Short and Sweet

Lord, guide me into all truth as I study Your holy word. Renew my mind concerning preaching and help me proclaim the good news daily. Amen.

Meditate and Memorize

"Then Philip opened his mouth, and beginning at this Scripture, preached Jesus to him."
—Acts 8:35

Believe and Receive

I am called to preach.

Listen and Learn

Identify any resistance you have to preaching.

_____
_____
_____
_____
_____
_____
_____
_____
_____
_____
_____
_____
_____
_____
_____
_____
_____
_____
_____
_____
_____
_____
_____
_____
_____
_____
_____
_____
_____
_____

Create and Relate
Use this space to connect with God through creativity.

ACTS 9
DAY NINE

VISION

ὅραμα

horama

hor'-am-ah

sight;
something gazed at;
a supernatural spectacle divinely
granted in an ecstasy or in a sleep

When God called Jeremiah to be a prophet, He asked him, "Jeremiah, what do you see?"[29] Jeremiah's destiny was connected to his vision. *Seeing* is a critical component of establishing your identity in the kingdom of God. It is one of the most fascinating ways we communicate with the One who *sees* the end from the beginning. By definition, vision is "the act or power of sensing with the eyes; anticipating that which will or may come to be; an experience in which a person, thing, or event appears vividly or credibly to the mind, although not actually present, often under the influence of a divine agency."

I want to address vision in two ways in this chapter. First, as it relates to supernatural "sight" in the spirit realm. Second, as it pertains to God's plans and purposes for your life. The two intertwine to facilitate greater intimacy with God and to help you fulfill your destiny. Jesus is the Master of restoring sight to the blind. Ask Him to open your eyes as you read. Ask Him to remove the blinders that would keep you from seeing Him as He longs to be seen. Ask Him to reveal Himself to you in new ways. Ask Him to give you *His* vision for your life and to prepare you for all that He has for you.

God is preparing the earth for the return of Christ by releasing revelation to His people. He is making things known in supernatural ways. This should not surprise most Bible-believing Christians. Many of the prophets and patriarchs of our faith had vivid encounters with God through open visions and heavenly visitations.

> *Jesus is the Master of restoring sight to the blind.*

Have you ever experienced a vision from the Lord like Cornelius, Peter, Ananias, and Paul did in the book of Acts? Have you ever encountered God in a trancelike state? Have you ever received wisdom, direction, or revelation in a dream? Have you ever been divinely inspired to create or build something according to a specific set of instructions? These are all ways that God speaks to His people. Joel 2:28 says, "And it shall come to pass afterward that I will pour out My

---

[29] Jeremiah 1:11

Spirit on all flesh; your sons and your daughters shall prophesy, your old men shall dream dreams, your young men shall see visions." Prophecy, dreams, and visions are part of God's glorious plan to equip a church that will usher in the second coming of Christ. This is made possible as He pours out His Spirit on *all* flesh—that includes you and me.

There are two references to visions in the ninth chapter of Acts. In Acts 9:10, God gave Ananias a vision concerning Saul. Ananias was a disciple at Damascus, and *God spoke to him in a vision to give him direction* concerning Saul's healing. The second vision is one God gave to Saul. Acts 9:12 says, "And in a vision he has seen a man named Ananias coming in and putting his hand on him, so that he might receive his sight." Saul had been blinded on the road to Damascus. In this vision, God allowed Paul to *see with his spiritual eyes what he was incapable of seeing with his natural eyes.* These two men had nothing in common except that God had a purpose for both of their lives, and He revealed it to them in visions.

Visions from God are as unique and special as the people who receive them. A thorough study of visions in the Bible will confirm that Abraham, Jacob, Moses, Samuel, Nathan, Eliphaz, Isaiah, Jeremiah, Ezekiel, Nebuchadnezzar, Daniel, Amos, Zechariah, Paul, Ananias, Cornelius, Peter, John, and many others encountered God in this way. Throughout Scripture, visions are often accompanied by an audible voice from heaven, an appearance of angels or human beings, or the representation of God Himself. They occurred during the day, in the night, and in trances. Most of the time, there was a clear understanding of the vision or an interpretation by someone else. God is still meeting with people this way today. He wants to reveal His heart, His will, and His secrets to His friends.

An alternate perspective of vision relates to the hopes, dreams, and aspirations you have about your future. Your vision is essentially the image of your destiny that beckons you forward with passion and tenacity. Martin Luther King, Jr., famously declared, "I have a dream!" In other words, he had a vision of what America could be apart from racism and segregation. He was inspired by God to move in a direction that would cause that dream to come to pass. As a result, he lived a life of purpose that eventually culminated in the fruition of his vision.

Visionaries are often pioneers. They break new ground and make a way where there seems to be no way. One vision from God given to an individual who is faithful and obedient can change the world. One person who explores a dream and pursues a larger-than-life possibility burning within them can ignite multitudes with purpose and passion.

I lived for over three decades without an understanding of God's plan for my life. I chased one fruitless "dream" after another with very little progress, success, or fulfillment before I decided to fully live for God. I had plenty of "good ideas" for my life, but none of them satisfied the deeper ache and longing I felt in my soul. Once I

> *Visions from God are as unique and special as the people who receive them.*

wholeheartedly committed to serve the Lord, study His word, and seek Him through prayer and fasting, He began to give me literal visions of my future with Him. These glimpses are always much bigger than I could imagine or accomplish on my own. Sometimes they come in dreams and other times I have a deep, intuitive knowing about something. Occasionally, I see what appears to be a movie playing before me, or I see a picture in my mind's eye. I often receive instructions or "blueprints" as I am journaling and praying.

I started by asking questions like "Who am I, Lord, and why am I here?" I reasoned that if God is real and He loves me, then He must have something extraordinary for me to do in this life that will exalt His name. After all, He is a *super*natural God. His thoughts and ways are higher than mine.[30] He is the Ephesians 3:20 God: "Now to Him who is able to do exceedingly abundantly above all that we ask or think, according to the power that works in us . . . ." He is the 1 Corinthians 2:9 God: "Eye has not seen, nor ear heard, nor have entered into the

---

[30] Isaiah 55:9

heart of man the things which God has prepared for those who love Him." He is the Jeremiah 29:11 God: "'For I know the thoughts that I think toward you,' says the Lord, 'thoughts of peace and not of evil, to give you a future and a hope.'" He is the Jeremiah 33:3 God: "Call to Me, and I will answer you, and show you great and mighty things, which you do not know." I believed His promises, and I wanted Him to *show* me what He wanted me to do and be in this life.

In John 5:19-20, Jesus said, "Most assuredly, I say to you, the Son can do nothing of Himself, but what He sees the Father do; for whatever He does, the Son also does in like manner. For the Father loves the Son, and shows Him all things that He Himself does; and He will show Him greater works than these, that you may marvel." Jesus only did what he *saw* His Father do. He lived an intimate and disciplined life of prayer and obedience. He sought His Father for instruction and direction every step of the way. At twelve years old, Jesus asked His mother, "Why did you seek Me? Did you not know that I must be about My Father's business?"[31] The will of the Father was His first priority, and He would not allow anyone or anything to stand in the way of fulfilling it.

God the Father *showed* His Son what was on His heart. This is vision in its purest form. When we begin to see as the Father sees, we can partner with Him to bring heaven to earth. Our natural and spiritual eyes must be open to see what God is doing all around us at any given moment. Moses asked God to *show* Him His glory, and He did.[32] When we ask God to show us something about Himself or about His will in the earth, He delights in responding.

In Acts 9, Saul of Tarsus encountered God in a way that forever altered his destiny. He was threatening and murdering Christians before God stepped in and revealed Himself in a supernatural way on the road to Damascus. Saul was a sinner. He was legalistic. He was radical and relentless. He believed he was doing what was right, but in reality he was wrong. When the pure light and holy voice of Jesus met him that day,

---

[31] Luke 2:49

[32] Exodus 33:18

Saul lost his natural eyesight. I find it interesting that this man who would become one of the greatest missionaries, evangelists, and martyrs the world will ever know was *struck blind* by the very One who called him and had a vision for his life. Why did God choose to remove Saul's sight? *I believe it was an abrupt removal of a dead vision.* Saul had a selfish vision before he was blinded by Truth and given a vision from heaven. God had chosen him to impact generations of people who would follow in his footsteps.[33] Paul needed new vision to bring this to pass.

God wants all of His children to see what He sees. He created you uniquely and for a purpose. He wants to give you vision for your life and set you on fire with passion. Nothing compares to the joy that accompanies a life lived with intention for His glory. God's plan is much bigger than yours. He wants to intercept your agenda through a divine encounter with holy love and set your feet on the path *He* has for you. It will require complete dependence on Him to attain it. You will need His supernatural direction and wisdom to guide you. Prophecy, dreams, and visions are a critical part of that journey.

As you pursue God's great plan for your life, you will relate to Ananias at times and know that you are being used to bring healing to others. Sometimes you will feel like Saul, groping around in the dark with a glimmer of hope that the light will return soon. In any and every circumstance, it is the vision God has given you that will lead you forward against all odds.

> *If you can SEE it, you can BE it!*

Remember this: *If you can SEE it, you can BE it!* You will never rise any higher than the vision you have of yourself. God wants to give you a fresh perspective. He wants you to see things according to *His* perfect will—in the spirit realm and in the natural realm. It is up to you, however, to *accept* His vision for your life, *believe* in it, and *act* on it. As a result, you can live with a fiery zeal that will not be quenched. You can run this race with perseverance as the Apostle Paul did. Paul was a changed

---

[33] Acts 9:15

man after His sight was restored. It is impossible to view life through the eyes of God without living differently. Ask Him to give you new sight today. Then expect to hear Him say, as He did to Jeremiah, "You have seen well, for I am ready to perform My word."[34]

---

[34] Jeremiah 1:12

Pause and Reflect

Do you believe that God has a vision for your life? Do you believe that you can encounter Him through dreams and visions?

_____

_____

_____

_____

_____

_____

_____

_____

_____

_____

_____

_____

Raw and Real

Selfish ambition, worldly pursuits, and busy lives are preventing God's people from seeing through His eyes.

Short and Sweet

Father, I need Your vision for my life. Speak to me in supernatural ways and open my eyes to see what You see. Amen.

Meditate and Memorize

"And in a vision he has seen a man named Ananias coming in and putting his hand on him, so that he might receive his sight." —Acts 9:12

Believe and Receive

I once was blind, but now I see.

Listen and Learn
Ask God to give you a vision.

_____

_____

_____

_____

_____

_____

_____

_____

_____

_____

_____

_____

_____

_____

_____

_____

_____

_____

_____

_____

_____

_____

_____

_____

_____

_____

_____

_____

_____

_____

Create and Relate
Use this space to connect with God through creativity.

ACTS 10
DAY TEN

PRAY

προσεύχομαι

proseuchomai

pros-yoo'-khom-ahee

to worship;
to ask for something
earnestly or humbly

91

One of the most important lessons I have learned concerning prayer involves two verses of Scripture. First, James 5:16 says, "The effective, fervent prayer of a righteous man avails much." Then 2 Corinthians 5:21 tells me, "For He made Him who knew no sin to be sin for us, that we might become the righteousness of God in Him." Because I have been made righteous through the atoning blood of Jesus, I can stand before the throne of glory and petition the Father with absolute confidence. I can rest assured that my prayers are not only being heard, but they are also powerful. This promise applies to every believer.

Without prayer, we cannot communicate with God. It is the avenue by which people from every tribe, tongue, and nation interact with the One who created them. The God of the universe has chosen to link arms with His children through prayer and the power of the Holy Spirit to accomplish His Kingdom purposes.

So what is prayer and why is it such a critical aspect of the Christian life? First and foremost, prayer is the way we speak with God and the way we listen to Him. It is the way we worship and petition Him. It is an open door to expression, allowing us to share our hearts and minds with the One who created us and knows us best. Prayer is as much a blessing to the one who is offering it as it is to a loving God who is receiving it. Prayer softens the heart of the one praying, and it releases a deeper understanding of who God is. When prayers are answered, faith is increased and lives are changed forever. An active prayer life essentially confirms the existence of a personally connected, intimately interested Creator.

When you spend time in prayer, you are nurturing the most important relationship in your life. Jesus was God in the flesh, and He still prayed. Not only did He pray, but He also portrayed a *lifestyle* of prayer. Mark 1:35 says, "Now in the morning, having risen a long while before daylight, He went out and departed to a solitary place; and there He prayed." Jesus was in constant communion with His Father through prayer. He emulated everything His Father said and did.[35] In John 14:9, Jesus said, "He who has seen Me has seen the Father." Imagine

---

[35]   John 5:19, 8:28

how different our lives, our churches, and our world would be if we truly followed Him in this way.

Acts 10 identifies Cornelius and Peter as men of prayer. Acts 10:2 says that Cornelius "prayed to God always." Verse 10:4 goes on to say that God remembered his prayers. Prayer was not only a daily discipline for Cornelius; it was an aspect of his character and nature. It was his lifestyle. Peter was also a man of great commitment to prayer. He recognized that only through constant communication with God would he be able to fulfill his purpose and do the greater works that Jesus commanded.[36] Because of their prayer lives, God gave both of these men visions; then He supernaturally connected them to one another. As a result of their obedience in prayer, the bonds of discrimination were broken and an entire household was saved, filled with the Holy Spirit, and then baptized with water. As we see with Cornelius and Peter, God clearly *speaks* and *releases visions and visitations* to His faithful ones through prayer.

Prayer is a matter of living in God's presence, being open and vulnerable with Him, trusting Him, and waiting on Him. Prayer is the perfect opportunity to get raw and real with God. No fake, phony stuff. Tell Him what is *really* on your heart and mind. He knows it anyway. Try not to approach God like He lives in another galaxy and do not believe the lie that He is too busy for you. He is an ever-present, loving Lord and Savior who hears the cries of your heart and longs to respond to them according to *His* perfect will and timing.

> *Jesus was God in the flesh, and He still prayed.*

Prayer is a two-way conversation with God. Sometimes you talk. Sometimes you listen. Prayers can be slight whispers of the heart in a moment of desperation or an elaborate profession of adoration regarding the majesty of God. Prayers are as unique and diverse as God's children. There is no set formula or list of things to say in order to pray "correctly." A friend of mine advises people who ask him how to pray to "begin by

---

[36] John 14:12

asking for *help* every morning, and end by saying *thank you* every night." How beautifully simple, yet powerful and effective! Prayer is an intimate connection between your heart and God's that is expressed in a variety of ways.

In 1 Thessalonians 5:17, Paul reminds us to "pray without ceasing." How do we do that? *We live in a perpetual state of acknowledgement that God is with us always and everywhere.* There is never a separation or distinction between our presence and His. A daily awareness and acceptance of this will fuel the fire of pursuit through prayer that fosters intimacy with God.

Have you ever had a thought, hope, or desire in your heart, but you never actually verbalized it? Then, to your great surprise, you received an "answer" to this "prayer" that you did not even realize you prayed? I have a friend who calls this *"prinking."* It falls somewhere between praying and thinking. God is so good that He will bless you with an answer to an unspoken prayer just to let you know that He cares about the tiniest details concerning your life.

Prayer is your opportunity to interact with God, personally and privately. What are you passionate about? What is on your mind? How do you *really* feel? For what or whom are you grateful? What are your greatest needs and desires? What do you love about God? How would you talk with your best friend? Who do you want God to heal or set free? Of what do you need to repent? What do you want to know about Jesus or His word? In what areas do you need wisdom or guidance? How can He *help*? Prayer is the key that unlocks God's heart. Do not forget to ask Him how *He* feels and what is on *His* heart as well. One of my favorite questions in prayer is, "What may I do for YOU today, Lord?"

God is forever the great I AM. He is the All-Sufficient One. He is more than enough. Connecting with Him in prayer opens the heavens over your life. Prayer fortifies your relationship with Him while increasing your knowledge and understanding of Him. It allows you to enter into His strength and joy, enabling you to endure any trial and weather every storm. Prayer ultimately releases God's kingdom on earth and establishes His will, both individually and corporately.

Jesus reminds us in Matthew 6:8, "For your Father knows the things you have need of before you ask Him." He then gives us a simple model to follow known as *The Lord's Prayer*.[37] This beautiful prayer consists of a mere 66 words, yet it addresses some of the most necessary components of walking with God. First, it refers to God as a Holy Father and identifies heaven as His abode. It mentions His kingdom and His will, along with a request for life-giving sustenance. Forgiveness, temptation, and deliverance are also addressed. The prayer closes with worship and exaltation. This command by Christ to pray in a specific manner reveals the importance of prayer, but it also lets us know that we do not have to be elaborate in our choice of words. God knows the heart of every individual on the planet. Regardless of how "qualified" you may or may not feel, your Father in heaven longs to hear your voice in prayer.

Revival truly begins in the heart of one person who learns the value of prayer; then it blazes forth into the earth as God releases answers to the effective, fervent prayers of His righteous ones. Christians in the Acts 29 church will be known as people of prayer. They will walk intimately with God in a relationship that is based upon communication with Him. Acts 10:38 says, "God anointed Jesus of Nazareth with the Holy Spirit and with power, who went about doing good and healing all who were oppressed by the devil, for God was with Him." *Doing good* and *healing all*—this is the fruit of a life given to intentional communion with God through prayer. Have you talked to Him today?

> *Prayer is the key that unlocks God's heart.*

---

[37] Matthew 6:5-13

Pause and Reflect

How faithful are you in your prayer life? What did you learn from Cornelius and Peter about the importance of praying without ceasing?

_____

_____

_____

_____

_____

_____

_____

_____

_____

_____

_____

_____

Raw and Real

Prayer is often a last resort instead of the first priority.

Short and Sweet

Oh, Lord, teach me how to pray. Use my prayers to change the world for Your glory. I want to live a lifestyle of prayer and intimacy with You. Amen.

Meditate and Memorize

"The next day, as they went on their journey and drew near the city, Peter went up on the housetop to pray, about the sixth hour."

—Acts 10:9

Believe and Receive

Prayer is a priority in my life.

Listen and Learn
Converse with God through prayer.

_____
_____
_____
_____
_____
_____
_____
_____
_____
_____
_____
_____
_____
_____
_____
_____
_____
_____
_____
_____
_____
_____
_____
_____
_____
_____
_____
_____
_____
_____
_____
_____
_____

Create and Relate
Use this space to connect with God through creativity.

ACTS 11
DAY ELEVEN

GRACE

χάρις

charis

khar'-ece

good will, loving-kindness, favor;
the divine influence upon the heart;
acceptable, benefit, gift, joy;
liberality, pleasure, thanks

Growing up, I often heard my mother and grandmother say, "There, but for the grace of God, go I." We definitely do not deserve to spend eternity with a holy God, but His amazing grace makes a way for us to be in His presence forever. Ephesians 2:8 says, "For by grace you have been saved through faith, and that not of yourselves; it is the gift of God . . . ." Grace is the door that stands open to all of God's children, beckoning them into His magnificent kingdom.

Grace is a word that is used often in Christendom, but what does it really mean? We sing about it, pray for it, and even "say grace" before meals. I spent a significant amount of time talking with God about "grace" as I began to write and review this chapter. I realized that my own understanding was elementary. I wanted to know more. I really wanted to take ownership of this concept of grace.

In my study, one particular passage of scripture moved me deeply, allowing God to reveal Himself to me in a very tangible and practical way. This is the type of encounter that is truly needed if we are to grow in our knowledge of who God is. He delights in our questions. He longs to see us mature in our walk with Him. As I meditated on 2 Corinthians 12:8-10, I received a fresh revelation of the grace of God. In his letter to the church at

> *"My grace is sufficient for you."*
>
> *2 Corinthians 12:9*

Corinth, the Apostle Paul wrote, "Concerning this thing I pleaded with the Lord three times that it might depart from me. And He said to me, 'My grace is sufficient for you, for My strength is made perfect in weakness.' Therefore most gladly I will rather boast in my infirmities, that the power of Christ may rest upon me. Therefore I take pleasure in infirmities, in reproaches, in needs, in persecutions, in distresses, for Christ's sake. For when I am weak, then I am strong." Beloved, no matter the trial or tribulation, despite the circumstances, regardless of the difficulty, HIS GRACE IS SUFFICIENT!

The word for *infirmities* in that passage refers to weakness, sickness, or disease in the body or soul. The human soul is comprised of the mind, will, and emotions. Whether you are facing a physical challenge, fighting a battle in your mind, or wrestling with an emotionally stressful situation, God wants to reveal His grace to you. I do not know what your weakness is or where you struggle the most, but God does. I cannot see into your soul or hear your innermost thoughts and concerns, but God can. *His* strength is revealed in your weakness, and His *grace* is all you need. Then you can "boast" and "take pleasure" in your troubles, as Paul did, "for Christ's sake." That simply means that when the human flesh is weak, God's glory becomes evident in supernatural ways. Rather than grumble or complain about our hardships, we should rejoice by faith that He *will* get the glory!

In Acts 10, Peter learned a powerful lesson concerning grace. The Jews argued with him regarding the topic of salvation for the Gentiles. Historically, the Jewish people exhibited extreme prejudice toward the Gentiles. They considered them unclean and referred to them as "dogs." This proverbial expression was used by the Jews to imply a sense of superiority over other "impure" nations. It was actually unlawful for an orthodox Jew to keep company with a Gentile. However, God gave Peter (a Jewish man) a vision in Acts 10 that convinced him that he should not call *anyone* common or unclean. The implications of this vision had such a profound impact on him that in Acts 10:34-35, Peter said, "In truth I perceive that God shows no partiality. But in every nation whoever fears Him and works righteousness is accepted by Him." Through one powerful encounter with God, Peter recognized that Jesus Christ died for all people, including the Gentiles. Years of wrong thinking were abandoned in a moment as he experienced the love and grace of God in a new way.

God began to pour out His Holy Spirit on the Gentiles. This astonished the Jews because they did not believe that God could bless anyone who was outside of the Abrahamic covenant. They were baffled when the Gentiles began speaking in other tongues. This was the same sign God had given the Jews on Pentecost as evidence that they had received the Holy Spirit. In Acts 11:15-17, Peter said, "And as I began to speak, the Holy Spirit fell upon them, as upon us at the beginning. Then I remembered the word of the Lord, how He said, 'John indeed baptized with water, but you shall be baptized with the Holy Spirit.' If therefore God gave them the same gift as He gave us when we believed on the Lord Jesus Christ, who was I that I could withstand God?" God was humbling His people and teaching them about Himself all at the same time. He wanted them to be free to love as He loves. Radical love requires radical grace. It crosses all racial, cultural, ethnic, and intellectual barriers.

Extreme prejudice runs rampant in the world today. From the elite to the street, there are people everywhere who judge, criticize, mock, and ridicule others. Discrimination is around every corner. Sometimes it is based on skin color or ethnicity. Other times it is sparked by a cultural difference or personality trait. Socioeconomic conditions and variances in lifestyles often bring more division than unity among people. As Christians, we are called to love God and love others. We are expected to be carriers of His grace as Peter was. There is no room for "holier-than-thou" hypocrisy in the Acts 29 church. We must completely conform to the Spirit of God so that the reality of His presence will invade the lives of everyone we meet. This is grace in action.

The grace of God humbles the human heart and releases an atmosphere of gratitude for the believer who truly understands and receives it. The Greek word for grace, *charis*, is derived from the word *chairō*. *Chairō* means to be full of cheer, calmly happy, or well off. Acts 11:23 says, "When he came and had seen the grace of God, he was glad, and encouraged them all that with purpose of heart they should continue with the Lord." Barnabas was happy when he saw that the Greek-speaking Christian men from Cyprus and Cyrene were extending God's grace to the Hellenists in Antioch. In this particular verse, it is believed that the Hellenists were Greek Gentiles rather than Greek-speaking Jews. At the time, Antioch was well known for

> *Radical love requires radical grace.*

its lack of morality, including Greek cults and ritual prostitution, but it would soon become a birthing ground for Gentile Christianity. These faithful evangelists were unaware of Peter's vision and testimony when they preached the gospel in Antioch. They simply moved forth with boldness to declare God's word to the Gentile unbelievers. They, too, wanted the Gentiles to experience salvation. People were beginning to understand God's grace in a way that brought Barnabas great joy.

Acts 11:21 reveals, "And the hand of the Lord was with them, and a great number believed and turned to the Lord." In the book of Acts, a revelation of grace caused a revival among the Gentiles. It also brought great freedom to the believing Jews, as they discovered the true purpose of the death, burial, and resurrection of Jesus. The grace of God sets *all* captives free!

Genesis 6:8 says, "But Noah found grace in the eyes of the Lord." There is grace in His gaze. As He looks at you, He longs to bestow His grace on you. As you gaze back at Him, there will be a willing and loving acceptance of that life-changing grace. As you come face-to-face with Grace Himself, you will gain a greater understanding of His love and compassion towards all people. Like Peter and Barnabas, you will become a conduit of God's grace and learn to recognize it when you see it in others.

I have heard that G.R.A.C.E. is *God's Riches at Christ's Expense.* Grace is essentially God's unmerited favor bestowed on sinful men and women. The grace of God is a gift. It is sovereign, secure, and strong. In your greatest time of need, grace will sustain you. When you are ready to give up, grace will enable you to finish strong. The glorious grace of God will empower and equip you to be who God has called you to be. When you are weak, He is strong. That is grace.

Titus 2:11-14 says, "For the grace of God that brings salvation has appeared to all men, teaching us that, denying ungodliness and worldly lusts, we should live soberly, righteously, and godly in the present age, looking for the blessed hope and glorious appearing of our great God and Savior Jesus Christ, who gave Himself for us, that He might redeem us from every lawless deed and purify for Himself His own special people, zealous for good works." The grace of God saves us and teaches us how to live lives of holiness and integrity according to God's word. His grace alone helps us survive in a broken world, as we wait with expectation for the return of Christ.

The Bible is clear that grace is an aspect of *who God is.* It is His very nature and identity. Apart from His grace, we would fumble around in the dark all of our days, searching for the meaning of life. We would constantly feel the eternal void that exists outside of a relationship with our loving Creator.

The grace of God chooses you to be His own. It allows you to stand against sin, grants you life and favor, and makes you profitable in every way. Grace answers you when you cry, upholds you when you slip or fall, and comforts your soul. The grace of God enabled Peter, and many other Jews, to embrace the Gentiles. Only by His grace are we able to love others, especially those so radically different from ourselves, as He loves us. Ask for a revelation of His grace today; then share it with someone else.

Pause and Reflect

Would people say that you are gracious? Are you willing to let God shatter your religious paradigms with His grace, as Peter was? How has God's grace changed your life?

_____

_____

_____

_____

_____

_____

_____

_____

_____

_____

Raw and Real

Prejudice within the church is preventing salvation from reaching unbelievers.

Short and Sweet

Gracious and loving Father, thank You for Your grace that is sufficient for me at all times and in all things. Give me a greater understanding of Your grace each day and help me reveal it to others. Amen.

Meditate and Memorize

"When he came and had seen the grace of God, he was glad, and encouraged them all that with purpose of heart they should continue with the Lord."
—Acts 11:23

Believe and Receive

God's grace is sufficient for me.

Listen and Learn

Thank God for His amazing grace.

_____
_____
_____
_____
_____
_____
_____
_____
_____
_____
_____
_____
_____
_____
_____
_____
_____
_____
_____
_____
_____
_____
_____
_____
_____
_____
_____
_____
_____
_____

Create and Relate
Use this space to connect with God through creativity.

ACTS 12
DAY TWELVE

ARISE

ἀνίστημι

anistēmi

an-is'-tay-mee

bring forward;
to cause to appear;
to cause to be born;
to lift, raise, or stand up;
to prepare for a journey

Acts 12 is a fascinating chapter. It reveals the undeniable humanity of Peter, the doubt and unbelief of the praying church, and the supernatural power of a loving, just God. Imagine this scenario with me for a moment. King Herod has just murdered James, the brother of John. Herod is a relentless, egotistical ruler who is seeking the approval of man. After witnessing the response of the Jews to the murder of James, Herod also arrests Peter and puts him in prison with the intention of killing him after Passover. Peter is being held in prison while the church fervently prays for a miracle. The night that Herod plans to murder Peter, an angel of the Lord appears to Peter in prison and commands him to "Arise quickly!" Now pause right there.

Put yourself in Peter's shoes. A man who is clearly not afraid to take a human life arrests you. You are placed in a prison under the supervision of four squads of soldiers. [A squad consisted of four Roman soldiers, two were confined with the prisoner and two kept guard outside. Sixteen soldiers were required to guard one prisoner all night, one squad for each of the four night watches.] You are bound with chains between two Roman soldiers, and this is the day that has been marked as your last day on earth. My question to you is this: What are you thinking and how are you feeling? Would you be sleeping like Peter or wide awake in a panic, consumed by fear and anxiety?

Peter may have been bound literally and physically in that prison on the evening of his appointed assassination, but he was eternally free in his heart. I am certain that he was abiding under the shadow of the Almighty and finding refuge beneath God's wings in his darkest hours.[38] I am convinced that it was the promises of God, written on his heart, combined with the faithful prayers of the church, which allowed him to rest in that prison cell. In fact, he was resting so well that when an angel of the Lord appeared to him, accompanied by a brilliant heavenly light, Peter still did not wake up! I marvel at the thought of this angel being forced to strike Peter on the side and raise him up to get his attention. How many of us would be sleeping that deeply in such dire circumstances?

---

[38]   Psalm 91

The Bible is not clear regarding Peter's thoughts in that prison cell. We do not know for sure if he accepted his death sentence and prepared for the worst or if he steadfastly believed that God would come to his rescue. Either way, he clearly resolved in his heart that whatever the Lord's will was, it was perfect. Hence his ability to sleep, deeply I might add, on that fateful night. Total surrender to the will of God will allow you to rest in any situation, regardless of the outcome.

What happened next speaks volumes. An angel of the Lord directed Peter to "Arise quickly!" In that moment, *the chains fell from Peter's hands.* Beloved, allow me to remind you that when God speaks, things happen! When God moves, shackles are broken and people are set free! Acts 12:5 says, "Peter was therefore kept in prison, but constant prayer was offered to God for him by the church." Peter's release was a direct answer to the prayers of those who were gathered at Mary's house interceding for him.

> *Total surrender to the will of God will allow you to rest in any situation, regardless of the outcome.*

Multitudes of people around the world are bound in chains and have lost all hope. They are confined to various prison cells of addiction, immorality, fear, depression, sickness, mental torment, and isolation. Doubt, disbelief and a myriad of other strongholds are preventing them from experiencing the miraculous freedom God promises in His word. We have a responsibility to pray for them, as the church in Acts 12 prayed for Peter.

Far too many people are sitting in church pews, chained to the enemy in some form or fashion. Perhaps you are one of them. If not, I can guarantee that you know someone who is. People you see on a regular basis need you to pray for their deliverance. As believers pray, angels are being sent out to do the work of the Lord. God wants to set the captives free! He is calling all of His children to "ARISE QUICKLY" and walk out of their confining, debilitating prisons.

"Prison" can refer to degenerate mindsets as well as literal captivity. In Romans 12:2, Paul instructs believers, "And do not be conformed to this world, but be transformed by the renewing of your mind, that you may prove what is that good and acceptable and perfect will of God." Like the Israelites wandering in the desert, you can be physically *set* free, yet still be in bondage if your mind is not renewed to the truth of God's word. Jesus said, "If you abide in My word, you are My disciples indeed. And you shall know the truth, and the truth shall make you free."[39] When you allow God to renew your mind daily, you will truly be *made* free. The Bible contains a solution to every problem you will ever face. However, it is up to you to seek the answers.

Peter did not ask a lot of questions the night the angel appeared to him in prison. He may have missed his window of opportunity if he had stopped to overanalyze or intellectualize what was happening. Proverbs 3:5 says, "Trust in the Lord with all your heart, and lean not on your own understanding." When God shows up and delivers us from captivity, He does it in miraculous ways. He does it so that we can share the testimony of His faithfulness with others. He does it in response to the prayers of His devoted servants. He does it to give us a greater understanding of who He really is. He does it because He *loves* us.

> *Peter's freedom was directly connected to his swift obedience.*

The only thing Peter was required to do in that prison cell was obey. The angel even helped him rise up. Peter's freedom was the direct result of his swift obedience. I do not know what your struggle is or what battle is before you at this moment, but I do know that obedience to the voice of the Lord will usher in your breakthrough. God will give you everything you need to endure the most difficult trials in your life. He will never leave you or forsake you, and He is always right on time. Like Peter, you must trust and obey Him in all things.

---

[39] John 8:31-32

I have heard it said that God is often an "eleventh hour" deliverer. I joke about Him being an "eleventh hour and fifty-ninth minute" deliverer. Sometimes you will truly wonder where God is and if He has forgotten you. Do not fear. He is with you. *He uses desperation to stretch us.* He teaches us through hardships and adversity that we can trust Him and that His plans for us are good.

Now imagine with me again that you are Peter. You are following a heavenly being as you are supernaturally led out of bondage and into freedom. You are a bit confused about the reality of it all, but you know that anything is better than being in that prison cell. The angel leads you to safety then departs from you. As you stand there wondering what to do next, how are you feeling? Are you elated that you are free or are you so concerned with the unknown details of your future that you long to go back into prison? When God delivers you, it is for a greater purpose. The human nature often wants to return to what was comfortable, familiar, or at least predictable, when there is uncertainty about the future. Do not look back. Keep moving forward.

John 8:36 says, "Therefore if the Son makes you free, you shall be free indeed." Jesus died for your freedom. Trust Him in all things and at all times as Peter did. Rest in the absolute assurance that He is with you and has your best interests in mind. In trust and rest, you will discover new levels of freedom that you have never known.

God is inviting you to follow Him out of captivity. He wants to get the glory out of your story. He wants to prove His eternal love for you. You are not forgotten. Awake from your slumber to see His glorious light shining into the deep darkness of your prison cell. Arise quickly and walk out of your confinement. Abide in His word, allow Him to renew your mind and be made free in the name of Jesus! Then go tell others how good God is.

Pause and Reflect

Where does the enemy have you bound in chains? How has the story of Peter's deliverance from prison impacted your faith and trust in God?

_____

_____

_____

_____

_____

_____

_____

_____

_____

_____

Raw and Real

Many people prefer to sleep in prison than put forth the effort to arise and walk out.

Short and Sweet

Thank You, Lord, for being the great Deliverer that You are. Lead me out of bondage and into Your perfect truth in every area of my life. Help me trust and rest in You all of my days. Amen.

Meditate and Memorize

"Now behold, an angel of the Lord stood by him, and a light shone in the prison; and he struck Peter on the side and raised him up, saying 'Arise quickly!' And his chains fell off his hands."
—Acts 12:7

Believe and Receive

The truth will make me free.

Listen and Learn
Ask God to help you arise quickly.

Create and Relate
Use this space to connect with God through creativity.

ACTS 13
DAY THIRTEEN

JUSTIFIED

δικαιόω

dikaioō

dik-ah-yo'-o

to be freed;
to render innocent;
to show one to be righteous

The word *justified* carries the connotation of giving an account or explanation for something. It conjures up thoughts of vindication and implies defense. How does this word affect a Christian's identity? What does a legal term have to do with the relationship we enter into with God through the salvation experience? It is imperative to gain a personal understanding of the definition and magnitude of this word as it relates to what Jesus did on the cross for each of us.

The Christian theological definition of justified is "to free from blame or declare guiltless; to make righteous in the sight of God." The legal definition is "to prove qualified as surety." Surety suggests the payment of a debt, for example, by someone who does not owe it. It indicates a person taking responsibility for someone else's performance or obligation. This is what Jesus did. He took our sins upon Himself. He paid a debt that He did not owe. He guaranteed that we would be absolved from all blame. His sacrifice assures us that we are qualified to stand before a holy God.

The word *justified* is used twice in Acts 13:39. Paul delivered his discourse on the Sabbath to the Jews at Antioch in Pisidia. After a somewhat lengthy exhortation, he closed with this declaration: "Therefore let it be known to you, brethren, that through this Man is preached to you the forgiveness of sins; and by Him everyone who believes is justified from all things from which you could not be justified by the law of Moses."[40] Paul realized the importance of explaining to the Jews what it means to be justified. He knew that men could not be acquitted from *all* of their guilt through the law of Moses. The stain of sin can only be removed through faith in Jesus Christ. Paul had personally experienced this liberty, and He wanted others to know the truth as well.

Romans 3:22-26 tells us that the righteousness of God is revealed ". . . through faith in Jesus Christ, to all and on all who believe. For there is no difference; for all have sinned and fall short of the glory of God, being justified freely by His grace through the redemption that is in Christ Jesus, whom God set forth as a propitiation by His blood, through faith, to

---

[40] Acts 13:38-39

demonstrate His righteousness, because in His forbearance God had passed over the sins that were previously committed, to demonstrate at the present time His righteousness, that He might be just and the justifier of the one who has faith in Jesus." I encourage you to pause and reflect on that passage of scripture for a moment. Talk with God about it and consider what it means for you personally.

> *The stain of sin can only be removed through faith in Jesus Christ.*

Many people profess a faith in Jesus without a real comprehension of what He did for them. God brought mankind into a right and real relationship with Himself through the crucifixion of Christ. His death on the cross completely destroyed the guilt of the sinner and satisfied the justice of God at the same time. Imagine how much freedom people will enjoy when they let go of all guilt and shame. Without a revelation of being made completely innocent in the sight of God, a sense of unworthiness prevents true intimacy from developing.

I spent many years bringing up "already forgiven" sins from my past in my prayer life. I will never forget the day the Lord interrupted me, "Jodi, I don't know what you are talking about." I immediately thought of Psalm 103:12, "As far as the east is from the west, so far has He removed our transgressions from us." I also remembered Micah 7:19, "You will cast all our sins into the depths of the sea," implying that they cannot be retrieved. Although I did not have language for it at the time, I realized that I had been justified. The moment I placed my faith in Christ, it was "just as if I'd" never done anything wrong. Isaiah 1:18 says, "Though your sins are like scarlet, they shall be as white as snow." We do not need to remind God of the past or meditate on guilt. Jesus died to set us free!

The blood of Christ is the atoning sacrifice for sin. The shedding of His blood replaced the Old Testament need for the blood of animals to be sprinkled on the mercy seat as reparation for sin. It is no longer the blood of an animal, but the blood of the sinless, spotless Lamb of God that makes a way for us to enter the Most Holy Place of God's presence. Apart from His blood, we would be eternally separated from a pure and holy God. However, because a believer has been justified, he or she can commune with Him forever. What gift could be greater?

The Apostle Paul and James, the half-brother of Jesus, both discussed justification in Scripture. In Romans 4:3, Paul referred to Abraham as being *justified by faith*. He quoted Genesis 15:6, which says, "Abraham believed God, and it was accounted to him for righteousness." Before he was circumcised or did anything to prove his faith, Abraham *believed* God. He believed God's promise to give him descendants through a biological child, even in his old age. Because of his unwavering faith in the face of impossible odds, God called him righteous. James also quoted Genesis 15:6, but he used it to assert that Abraham was *justified by works*.[41] James 2:21 says, "Was not Abraham our father justified by works when he offered Isaac his son on the altar?" So which is it? Are we justified by faith or justified by works?

The answer is *both*. We are justified by faith before God and by works before men. Abraham was justified by faith before God the moment he believed. He was justified by works before men when he *demonstrated* his faith by offering Isaac as a sacrifice on the altar.[42] Abraham *acted* on his faith when he obeyed the voice of God. This is why James goes on to say in James 2:22-24, "Do you see that faith was working together with his works, and by works faith was made perfect? And the Scripture was fulfilled which says, 'Abraham believed God, and it was accounted to him for righteousness.' And he was called the friend of God. You see then that a man is justified by works, and not by faith only."

It is impossible to have faith in Christ without yielding works. Although our works add nothing to our righteousness, they prove to others that our faith is alive. This is confirmed in James 2:14-18, "What does it profit, my brethren, if

---

[41]   James 2:23
[42]   Genesis 22

someone says he has faith but does not have works? Can faith save him? If a brother or sister is naked and destitute of daily food, and one of you says to them, 'Depart in peace, be warmed and filled,' but you do not give them the things which are needed for the body, what does it profit? Thus also faith by itself, if it does not have works, is dead. But someone will say, 'You have faith, and I have works.' Show me your faith without your works, and I will show you my faith by my works."

The Greek word for *works* is *ergon*, and it means toil, occupation, deed, labor, or act. We are justified before God by believing in the finished work of Christ on the cross, but we prove our faith before men by the evidence of our obedience. One of the greatest dangers of the doctrine of *justification by faith alone* is that people claim that they have been set free and then they continue to live ungodly lives. This is not what God intended. Justification does not leave you without responsibility, as Paul and James affirm. Instead, it should provoke and inspire you to live a life that reveals your faith to men by what you do.

Remember that your works alone will never place you in right standing before God. Justification cannot be earned. You do not have to fight for it or strive to receive it. It is finished. You will never be able to achieve the sinless perfection that Jesus did, and you cannot be made righteous through performance or good deeds. The righteousness that Jesus attained by living in complete obedience is accounted to you for righteousness. Being justified by faith means that God sees you through His blood when you put your reliance and trust in Christ. 2 Corinthians 5:21 says, "For He made Him who knew no sin to be sin for us, that we might become the righteousness of God in Him."

The righteousness of Christ is for all who believe. If you are a believer, you have been made innocent in the sight of God. We have the blood of Jesus to thank for this glorious freedom from guilt, shame, and unworthiness. All penalties of sin are eradicated through the shed blood of the Lamb of God.

Everyone who believes is justified from all things. *All* things. Justification is not merely offered to you, it is a cloak that covers you and a crown that identifies you as God's own. It is a free gift given to those who do not deserve it but who choose to receive it. The next time you find yourself feeling guilty for something that God has

> The righteousness of Christ is for all who believe.

already forgiven you for, remember this . . . It is *"just as if I'd"* never done anything wrong. Then thank God that you have been justified by the greatest Justifier the world has ever known.

Pause and Reflect

What does it mean to be justified? Do you feel differently about yourself and your relationship with God because of this revelation?

_____

_____

_____

_____

_____

_____

_____

_____

_____

_____

Raw and Real

Satan is winning the battle for freedom in many Christian lives because they do not know they have been justified.

Short and Sweet

Holy and righteous Father, please give me a greater understanding of what it means to be justified. Help me let go of all guilt and live with absolute confidence before You. Amen.

Meditate and Memorize

"Therefore, let it be known to you, brethren, that through this Man is preached to you the forgiveness of sins; and by Him everyone who believes is justified from all things which you could not be justified by the law of Moses."
—Acts 13:38-39

Believe and Receive

God sees me through the blood of Jesus.

Listen and Learn
Meditate on your innocence in Christ.

Create and Relate
Use this space to connect with God through creativity.

TURN

ἐπιστρέφω

epistrephō

ep-ee-stref'-o

to revert;
to bring back;
to be converted;
to cause to return

It has never been "cool" to be a Christian. Christianity did not begin with a "cool" factor, and I am certain that it will not end with one. Many of the disciples in the book of Acts were persecuted, threatened, and stoned because of their obedience in doing the Lord's work. It definitely was not "cool" to be a Christian in the early church. However, in recent decades, with the onset of media, entertainment, and the Internet, it has become more "popular" to be a Christian, particularly in the Western world, and particularly among the younger generation.

In my travels, I have noticed the vast differences between those who simply "identify" with Christianity and those who are "identified" as Christians. Just because you wear a t-shirt with a cross on it and know all of the contemporary worship songs does not mean that you exhibit the character and nature of Christ. By the same token, just because you have attended the same church for over fifty years and have a title next to your name in the bulletin, does not indicate that you are living a pure and holy life. 1 Samuel 16:7 reminds us, "For the Lord does not see as man sees; for man looks at the outward appearance, but the Lord looks at the heart."

> *It has never been "cool" to be a Christian.*

God sees what no one else sees. He gazes upon the heart of man and knows if the inside lines up with the outside. He knows if the t-shirt and the lyrics are truly a reflection of what is in the heart. He knows if a person's character and integrity are as presentable at home as they are on the church property. One way we can ensure that our lives are consistently in agreement with God's word is to remember daily to *turn*. Turn *away* from self and turn *to* God. Turn *away* from the fallen sinful nature and turn *to* the nature of Christ—with all meekness, humility, and love.

In Acts 14, Paul and Barnabas preached in Iconium and Lystra. Verse 3 says, "Therefore they stayed there a long time, speaking boldly in the Lord, who was bearing witness to the word of His grace, granting signs and wonders to be done by their hands." In Lystra, a crippled man who had never walked was miraculously healed through Paul's ministry. As a result, the people of that city began to worship Paul and Barnabas as though they were gods. Think about that. The Lycaonian citizens believed that these two men were Zeus and Hermes in the flesh. Why? What caused this great misunderstanding?

As we established in Chapter 6, *everyone places faith in something or someone.* The people of Lystra did not know the one, true God. They did not know Jesus Christ as their Savior and Redeemer. The inclination of their hearts was to worship, but it was misplaced because they had not received the truth. Paul's message in those moments is one that still speaks loudly and clearly today. In Acts 14:15 he said, "Men, why are you doing these things? We also are men with the same nature as you, and preach to you that you should turn from these useless things to the living God, who made the heaven, the earth, the sea, and all things that are in them . . . ." By warning them to turn, Paul was exhorting them to be converted, to love wisdom and righteousness, and to live differently. He was inviting them to experience and enjoy a real relationship with a living, loving God.

Did you know that the word *repent* actually means to *turn* away from something because of regret or remorse, to think differently, and to change one's mind for the better? It essentially refers to reconsidering something with an attitude that desires improvement. My observation is that many people live according to their own standards rather than according to God's. This is exactly what is happening around the world as people reject the truth on a daily basis. Romans 3:18 says, "There is no fear of God before their eyes." Proverbs 14:12 says, "There is a way that seems right to a man, but its end is the way of death." Romans 6:23 says, "For the wages of sin is death, but the gift of God is eternal life in Christ Jesus our Lord."

Sin is a dead-end road that I traveled down for thirty-one years before I decided to repent and turn from my selfish ways. Thankfully, according to Romans 5:20, ". . . where sin abounded, grace abounded much more . . . ." As soon as I turned, I found myself in the arms of love. My heavenly Father joyfully welcomed me home. In a moment, I was in right standing before the King of glory. Like the prodigal son, I had been out on a long, fruitless journey that was leading me towards eternal destruction. One simple decision to "turn" changed my life forever.

Forgiveness is a beautiful thing. No one is perfect, and God does not expect us to be. That is exactly why He sent Jesus to bear the cross and die for our sins. This life is a work in progress. In all of humanity, there has only been One who lived a sinless life, and that is Jesus. Romans 3:23 says, "... for all have sinned and fall short of the glory of God, being justified freely by His grace through the redemption that is in Christ Jesus ...." The guilty conscience that accompanies sin is only relieved as we are made righteous through the sacrificial death of Christ.

> *One simple decision to "turn" changed my life forever.*

That glorious sacrifice was made once and for all, but it does not stop there. There is a constant battle for each life on this planet. Ephesians 6:12 says, "For we do not wrestle against flesh and blood, but against principalities, against powers, against the rulers of the darkness of this age, against spiritual hosts of wickedness in the heavenly places." Light and darkness are warring over every soul day in and day out. With a little complacency or a crack in the foundation, Satan will come in like a flood. 1 Peter 5:8-9 advises us to "Be sober, be vigilant; because your adversary the devil walks about like a roaring lion, seeking whom he may devour. Resist him, steadfast in the faith, knowing that the same sufferings are experienced by your brotherhood in the world."

How do you resist your adversary? The first thing you do is *turn*. Make a conscious decision *not* to sin. Acts 14:2 says, "But the unbelieving Jews stirred up the Gentiles and poisoned their minds against the brethren." Satan will "stir up" other people and use them against you. He wants to poison minds with temptations, accusations, negativity, criticism and lies. He will attempt to seduce, entice, and allure you into his wicked ways by appealing to your emotions, cravings, and desires. Winning the war between your ears requires that you take every thought captive according to 2 Corinthians 10:3-6: "For though we walk in the flesh, we do not war according to the flesh. For the weapons of our warfare are not carnal but mighty in God for pulling down strongholds, casting down arguments and every high thing that exalts itself against the knowledge of God, bringing every thought into captivity to the obedience of Christ, and being ready to punish all disobedience when your obedience is fulfilled."

True change begins when you make a decision to walk away from darkness and enter into the glorious light of God. The word of God gives you everything you need to be victorious. Ephesians 6:13-18 says, "Therefore take up the whole armor of God, that you may be able to withstand in the evil day, and having done all, to stand. Stand therefore, having girded your waist with truth, having put on the breastplate of righteousness, and having shod your feet with the preparation of the gospel of peace; above all, taking the shield of faith with which you will be able to quench all the fiery darts of the wicked one. And take the helmet of salvation, and the sword of the Spirit, which is the word of God; praying always with all prayer and supplication in the Spirit, being watchful to this end with all perseverance and supplication for all the saints . . . ." A soldier would not go to war without protection. Neither should we.

In Acts 14, Paul instructed the people in Lystra to *turn from useless things.* The Greek word for useless in that verse is *mataios*, and it means empty, profitless, vain, and without purpose. How many people are seeking those very things today? In the process of resisting your adversary through spiritual warfare, God desires that you physically turn away from anything that is useless. Your Creator is very intentional. He did not place a single person on this planet without a purpose. When you waste your time seeking after, worshiping, or partaking in anything that is void of purity, holiness, life, or purpose, it becomes a vain and useless pursuit. Paul recognized this as the people in Lystra were bringing their sacrifices to him. They were chasing after useless gods, yet they were too stubborn and blind to see it. Paul was desperately pleading with them to *turn.* He knew the consequence of their sin would be death if they continued to reject the truth.

Sin is pleasurable. The Bible even tells us so in Hebrews 11:25, noting that Moses chose ". . . rather to suffer affliction with the people of God than to enjoy the passing pleasures of sin . . . ." Are those few moments of passing pleasure worth the tremendous price of death?

What do you need to turn from today? What are the vain pursuits that God wants you to cast off? Everyone has something that God is working on in his or her life at any given moment. If you are not a believer, He is working on your heart to reveal the truth to you. If you are a Christian, He is asking you to turn away from certain people, places, things, and attitudes that do not glorify Him. If He is leading you away from a particular lifestyle, habit, activity, person, thought process, etc., it is only because He has something better to offer you. God alone knows exactly what is required for you to fulfill your purpose on this earth. *Turning* is a necessary part of that journey.

Romans 4:7 says, "Blessed are those whose lawless deeds are forgiven, and whose sins are covered." Throughout the Bible, God reveals His grace, mercy, and blessings to those who turn from sin and seek His ways. He is holy; He is pure; and He is worthy of our best at all times. 2 Chronicles 7:13-15 says, "When I shut up heaven and there is no rain, or command the locusts to devour the land, or send pestilence among My people, if My people who are called by My name will humble themselves, and pray and seek My face, and turn from their wicked ways, then I will hear from heaven, and will forgive their sin and heal their land. Now My eyes will be open and My ears attentive to prayer made in this place." When you are prompted by the Holy Spirit to turn, do it quickly. As each of us turns from our wicked ways and useless things, God will

> *When you are prompted by the Holy Spirit to turn, do it quickly.*

hear, forgive, and heal. True identity will be restored. A wildfire of awakening will spread throughout our land. All it takes is just one spark.

Pause and Reflect

When was the last time you encouraged someone to "turn" as Paul did? How will you make an effort to be more sensitive to the guidance of the Holy Spirit in this area?

_____

_____

_____

_____

_____

_____

_____

_____

_____

Raw and Real

Turning *from* wickedness is only completed by turning *toward* holiness.

Short and Sweet

God, You are holy. Increase my sensitivity to Your voice as I grow in my relationship with You. Give me the courage and wisdom that I need daily to walk away from the pleasures of sin and turn from useless things. Amen.

Meditate and Memorize

"Men, why are you doing these things? We also are men with the same nature as you, and preach to you that you should turn from these useless things to the living God, who made the heaven, the earth, the sea, and all things that are in them."
—Acts 14:15

Believe and Receive

I will turn from useless things.

Listen and Learn
Ask God to reveal anything useless in your life.

_____

_____

_____

_____

_____

_____

_____

_____

_____

_____

_____

_____

_____

_____

_____

_____

_____

_____

_____

_____

_____

_____

_____

_____

_____

_____

_____

_____

_____

_____

_____

_____

_____

_____

_____

Create and Relate
Use this space to connect with God through creativity.

ACTS 15
DAY FIFTEEN

CONVERSION

ἐπιστροφή

epistrophē

ep-is-trof-ay'

a moral revolution

Can you remember the specific date of your conversion to Christianity? That moment is so profound and radically life-altering for many people that it becomes the most important day of their lives. This is exactly what happened to me on November 27, 2005, when I made the decision to surrender my life to Christ. I celebrate that day every year with fasting, prayer, and thanksgiving. I call it my "New Birth" Day. It is a day I will never forget, and it set my life in motion with a purpose and passion that I never knew was available to me.

My conversion from nonbeliever to believer was so real and tangible that there is simply no denying that it happened. As with the Apostle Paul on the road to Damascus, I encountered Jesus on that day so powerfully that it forever changed me. Ask anyone who knew me then and knows me now, and they will tell you that I am not the same person I was before I met Jesus. My life is a continual process of growing and discovering who I am in Him. I may not be who I hope to be, but I sure am glad I am not who I used to be!

Conversion is a journey that often begins with a single defining moment in a person's life. I have talked with many people who ponder the day they surrendered all, remembering it with renewed hope and a fresh joy. I have also met people who say they have been Christians all of their lives but are unable to pinpoint a specific day or time when everything changed. Still others say they vaguely remember the moment that they chose Christ. I want to provoke you to consider the implications of the word *conversion* today. By definition, it is the act of *changing* one's religion or beliefs. The Christian theological definition alludes to repentance and the process of *changing* to a godly life. In both of those definitions, the key word is *change*. It is impossible to be converted to Christianity without experiencing change.

Think about it from a different perspective for a moment. The word *conversion* is used to refer to food that is *changed* into energy or body tissue over time. It is also used to describe the *alteration* of a building for a new purpose, such as the conversion of a house into apartments. When you hear this word in modern culture, it suggests reshaping, reconstruction, and renewal. Some of the features or structures may remain the same, but the general idea is that something or someone is clearly transformed into a new creation. This is the Christian's conversion. It is a moral revolution, of sorts, that causes divine beauty to arise from filthy ashes.

The Greek word for *conversion* is actually derived from the word we studied in Chapter 14 for *turn*. If you look at both words in the Greek, you will notice the similarities. Why is this? It is because you cannot effectively experience a *conversion* apart from *turning* away from old sinful ways of living. Conversion requires the rejection of sin and a wholehearted commitment to live for the glory of God in every area of your life. It is the metaphorical metamorphosis of the caterpillar into the butterfly. It is the shedding of the old and stepping fully into the new, enabling one to reach spiritual heights previously unexplored. There is freedom in that place.

> *It is impossible to be converted to Christianity without experiencing change.*

The majority of Acts 15 focuses on the conflict over circumcision between the Jews and the Gentiles. Acts 15:1 says, "And certain men came down from Judea and taught the brethren, 'Unless you are circumcised according to the custom of Moses, you cannot be saved.'" Verse 5 also says, "But some of the sect of the Pharisees who believed rose up, saying, 'It is necessary to circumcise them, and to command them to keep the law of Moses.'" In their legalistic approach to salvation, the Jews were actually destroying the freedom that accompanies true Christianity. Rules, rules, and more rules will suck the life right out of a Christian. *God is after the heart.* Relationship trumps religion every time. When the human heart is sincerely converted, a follower of Christ longs to obey His word, enjoy His presence, be led by his Spirit, and grow in an authentic relationship with Him. Too many rules will occasionally send someone right back into sin. Jesus came to fulfill the law and set us all free! He loves us, and He longs to commune with us in a personal way each and every day. It is His *love* that compels a believer to live a holy life. When the hands are clean and the heart is pure, "rules" will be followed instinctively.[43] Any deviation from God's principles will grieve the heart of a truly converted Christian.

In Acts 15:3, the believers in Phoenicia and Samaria expressed "great joy" upon hearing about the conversion of the Gentiles. Do you rejoice when someone makes a decision to accept Jesus Christ as Lord and Savior? Do you get excited about the journey he or she is embarking on because you have experienced a *change* yourself? Are you able to relate with enthusiasm to another person's testimony? Do you thank God for their hopeful future because you know that abundant life only exists in a thriving relationship with Him? Once you taste the goodness of God, you will connect with others who know Him in a very special and unique way. You, too, will have "great joy" at the news of their salvation, and you will earnestly welcome them into your ever-growing family.

An authentic conversion from unbeliever to believer is noticeable by all. A convert for Christ will not think, act, or speak the same way he or she did prior to choosing to live for Him. Friends, family members, and coworkers will discern a very clear difference in the character and nature of a Christian who has genuinely been converted. As the years go by and the word of God begins to take root, the attitude and heart of Jesus become more apparent in the life of a believer. 2 Corinthians 5:17 declares the power of conversion: "Therefore, if anyone is in Christ, he is a new creation; old things have passed away; behold, all things have become new." *All things* become new as you surrender your life to Him daily.

> *An authentic conversion from unbeliever to believer is noticeable by all.*

Paul and Barnabas were on a mission to convert people to Christianity in Acts 15. Unfortunately, unbelievers are often resistant to evangelical Christians today. Many Bible-believing

---

[43]   Psalm 24:4

Christians also fear offending people when it comes to "religion." Why? Do we have the gift of eternal life to offer lost souls? Do we have the answer to every problem humanity will ever face? If you knew someone was dying and you had the cure for their condition, would you sit idly by and watch them waste away? This is happening all over the world as Christians live silent lives of "faith." Too many followers of Christ avoid sharing the gospel because they fear conflict or confrontation. However, when you have truly been converted, as Paul and the disciples were, you want to shout it from the rooftops. *He died to set you free!* That is indeed good news.

Pause and Reflect

Have you experienced a conversion to Christianity? If so, how has your life *changed* because of your conversion? If not, what is stopping you?

_____

_____

_____

_____

_____

_____

_____

_____

_____

_____

Raw and Real

Conversions are not confined to Sunday service during the altar call.

Short and Sweet

Jesus, thank You for dying for my sins. I want to live my life in such a way that people see You in me. Help me share the good news of the gospel with others. Amen.

Meditate and Memorize

"So, being sent on their way by the church, they passed through Phoenicia and Samaria; describing the conversion of the Gentiles; and they caused great joy to all the brethren."
—Acts 15:3

Believe and Receive

I am a new creation.

Listen and Learn
Identify the areas of your life that still need to change.

_____

_____

_____

_____

_____

_____

_____

_____

_____

_____

_____

_____

_____

_____

_____

_____

_____

_____

_____

_____

_____

_____

_____

_____

_____

_____

_____

_____

_____

_____

_____

_____

_____

_____

Create and Relate
Use this space to connect with God through creativity.

ACTS 16
DAY SIXTEEN

SERVANTS

δοῦλος

doulos

doo'-los

slave, bondman, attendant;
one who submits to another's will;
devoted to another to the disregard
of one's own interest

In a world where convenience and luxury have no bounds, the idea of *being served* has become much more popular than actually *serving*. In fact, people have been known to frown upon occupations that require true service. There is a "better than" attitude that people can exude toward those in positions of service, almost as if they "deserve" to be served.

Generally speaking, service-oriented occupations are often taken for granted. I personally witnessed this not long after I made the decision to surrender my heart and life to God. He directed me to take a job as a third shift waitress in a 24-hour fast food diner. It happened to be located in a college town next to a busy nightclub. The people I encountered during those hours were not your average restaurant patrons. They were often intoxicated, rowdy, and rude. They demanded what they wanted without regard to the implications of their sarcasm, selfishness, or arrogance. They definitely did not appreciate the service they received.

Interestingly, I moved from a position of leadership with a Fortune 500 Company, where I was making a six-figure income, into a position of service working for tips as I pursued greater intimacy with God. To this day, that was one of the most important and enlightening seasons of my life. Learning to lead by serving is humbling and empowering. I remember my first day at work, putting on my uniform, looking in the mirror, and saying, "Lord, if there was an ounce of pride left in me, it's gone now!" In His infinite wisdom, He knew there was an ounce still in there. As I was washing dishes that first night, a familiar gentleman approached the counter. I recognized his face, but I could not remember his name. I politely said, "I believe I know you. You look familiar." With an interesting look on his face, he ignored me as if to say, "I don't think so, lady." I continued to wash my dishes and talk to the Lord about this pride that was clearly still affecting me. I was apparently embarrassed by my new position of service. Finally, it hit me. The Lord reminded me how I knew this man. I looked him in the eyes and said, "Jim?!" In shock, he stared at my nametag, then at my face, then at my nametag, then at my face, and he exclaimed, "Jodi?!" I responded, "Jim?!" He shouted, "JODI?!" Then he proceeded to stand up and make the entire restaurant aware that "This lady used to be my boss!"

In a split second, any remaining pride was gone. In one moment, I was free to serve with no inhibitions. I had actually hired this man when I worked for the Fortune 500 Company. He did not live in the area. In fact, he lived several hours away. But God saw to it that he would be in *that* city, on *that* evening, eating at *that* diner, during my first night on the job. Thus began my journey as a humble servant.

That first week brought with it many interesting challenges. I was assigned to bathroom duty and had my cell phone stolen. As the "new girl," I also got the dirty jobs that no one else wanted—like cleaning up after an inebriated young lady who got sick in her booth. That job ranks as one of the most significant, transformational, and life-giving opportunities I have had the honor of accepting as a Christian. I learned to take the low road as Jesus did. I watched as people were flabbergasted by His peace and joy flowing through me during stressful times. Co-workers got saved and customers experienced the light and love of Christ. Most importantly, I was blessed to learn about the heart of God through hard-working, committed brothers and sisters as they served Him by serving others.

Serving is not for the faint of heart. It can be a dirty job, but it is one of the greatest blessings we have been given in this life. It is God's brilliant way of teaching us that it is not all about us. Fortunately, I was able to manage the difficult circumstances in that diner through the grace and strength of the Lord. However, many people become calloused or exhausted as they serve. Something is wrong with this picture. Serving someone else's needs, desires, or vision is actually liberating. It eradicates selfishness and reveals the true character of Christ. It opens blind eyes and renews narrow minds. It allows a follower of Christ to tangibly

> *Serving someone else's needs, desires, or vision is actually liberating.*

experience the essence of who He really is. The perfect love of God is shed abroad through the humble life of a servant.

The word *servants* in Acts 16 comes from the Greek word *doulos.* That same Greek word is translated as *slave* in Matthew 20:27-28 as Jesus instructed His disciples: "And whoever desires to be first among you, let him be your slave—just as the Son of Man did not come to be served, but to serve, and to give His life a ransom for many." Then in Philippians 2:7, *doulos* is translated as *bondservant.* Historically, a bondservant was someone who was held in a permanent position of servitude and was considered the owner's personal property. It also refers to someone who *chooses* to remain a servant after being given an opportunity for release. Paul makes it clear in Philippians 2:7 that Jesus ". . . made Himself of no reputation, taking the form of a bondservant, and coming in the likeness of men." The beauty of being a bondservant in the kingdom of God is that you live with a realization that you are free to go at any time. Yet you *choose* to stay, serving Him willingly, wholeheartedly, and gratefully all of your days. Most importantly, you do this out of love—pure, selfless, holy love.

So what exactly does it mean to be a servant today? The following italicized phrases from Acts 16 give us a bird's-eye view into true servanthood in the kingdom of God. Servants *recruit disciples to do God's work* (verse 3) and *are guided by the Holy Spirit* (verses 6-7). They *receive visions from the Lord and are directed to help others* (verse 9). They *share the gospel* (verses 10, 13, 31-32), *do not discriminate* (verse 13), *baptize new believers* (verse 15), *cast out demons* (verse 18), and *endure persecution* (verses 19, 22-24). Servants *pray and sing to God* (verse 25), *experience miracles, signs, and wonders* (verse 26), *are delivered from bondage* (verse 26), and *cause others to inquire about salvation* (verse 30). They *fellowship and celebrate with God's people* (verse 34), *speak boldly in the name of the Lord* (verse 37), and *encourage the brethren* (verse 40).

What do these descriptions of a servant have in common? They each require absolute abandonment of self and complete surrender to God. As Christians, we live in an upside-down kingdom where the low road leads to a high place. According to Jesus, greatness is not defined by the title behind your name, the diplomas hanging on your walls, the square footage of your home, or the number of zeros in your income. It is defined by your service. In Matthew 20:26, Jesus said, "Whoever desires to become great among you, let him be your servant." We want to become more like Jesus, and that is impossible without knowing Him as a Servant King.

I recently purchased a mobile phone that contains an electronic "servant" in its tiny little case. You can ask "her" anything, and she will respond. I could not believe my ears when I heard *"I live to serve"* come from the speaker of my phone one day. What?! True service can only flow from a *living* heart of compassion that desires to impart the pure love of God to another. If people truly comprehended the importance of personally and wholeheartedly serving one another in love, the world would be a much better place.

Everything from taking out the trash to leading a nation can be accomplished through the heart of a servant. Satan despises this heart posture because it reminds him of the everlasting love and compassion of God. In Acts 16:17-18, a slave girl possessed with the spirit of divination followed the disciples saying, "These men are the servants of the Most High God, who proclaim to us the way of salvation. And this she did for many days." Even the demon identified Paul and the brethren as servants!

> *"Whoever desires to become great among you, let him be your servant."*
>
> *Matthew 20:26*

A servant of the Most High God has the privilege of revealing Him to others through words, deeds, attitudes, and a life lived on purpose for His glory. Whether you are a soldier in the armed forces, a mortgage lender, a drive-through operator, or a volunteer at the local soup kitchen, your service matters. If you are a spouse, CEO, health care practitioner, or garbage truck driver, your service matters. If you spend your entire life on the mission field in a foreign land, teach children how to do something extraordinary, or commit your time to caring for an elderly parent, your service matters. Determine to live in such a way that you, too, are recognized as a servant of the Most High God. There is no greater honor.

We all want to hear those glorious words someday, "Well done, good and faithful servant."[44] As you humble yourself and place another's needs before your own, you are doing what Jesus would do. He sees it, and it shall be rewarded. Colossians 3:23-24 says, "And whatever you do, do it heartily, as to the Lord and not to men, knowing that from the Lord you will receive the reward of the inheritance; for you serve the Lord Christ." Do not merely pursue worldly pleasures, successes, or accolades. Seek eternal rewards and blessings from above. As an appointed leader in the kingdom of God, make it your mission to serve. Jesus left His throne in heaven to serve weak and mortal humans. The Acts 29 family of believers will follow in His footsteps.

---

[44] Matthew 25:23

Pause and Reflect

Do you think people recognize you as a servant? How will you be more intentional about serving God and others in the future?

_____

_____

_____

_____

_____

_____

_____

_____

_____

_____

_____

Raw and Real

Apart from love, service is mere duty.

Short and Sweet

Servant King, thank You for the humility You displayed when You came to earth to save my soul. Teach me how to be more like You and help me serve others as You would serve them. Amen.

Meditate and Memorize

"This girl followed Paul and us, and cried out, saying, 'These men are the servants of the Most High God, who proclaim to us the way of salvation.'"
—Acts 16:17

Believe and Receive

I am a servant of the Most High God.

Listen and Learn

Consider the ways that Jesus served.

_____
_____
_____
_____
_____
_____
_____
_____
_____
_____
_____
_____
_____
_____
_____
_____
_____
_____
_____
_____
_____
_____
_____
_____
_____
_____
_____
_____

Create and Relate
Use this space to connect with God through creativity.

OFFSPRING

γένος

genos

ghen'-os

born, diversity, generation;
kindred: family, stock, tribe, nation;
the aggregate of many individuals
of the same nature, kind, or sort

There is an identity crisis occurring in the lives of people all around the world. Satan is having his way with God's children as he lies to them about who they are, where they came from, and why they are here. He is leading precious souls into a bottomless pit of depression, loneliness, fear, and rebellion because they do not know the truth. He is deceiving hearts and minds daily with thoughts of being forgotten, forsaken, abandoned, neglected, and rejected by God and others. This is not the will of the Father for His beloved children.

A revelation of *who* you are and *whose* you are releases a breakthrough of power and purpose in your life. When you become aware of your identity in Christ as a blood-bought son or daughter of the King of Glory, your entire outlook and attitude about life changes. You no longer concern yourself with pleasing man, nor do you live devoid of value or worth. When you believe and accept that Jesus died for YOU, it completely and radically alters your approach to living. Even in the most difficult circumstances, the knowledge that you have a Heavenly *Father* who loves you establishes something within you that can never be shaken. This is foundational to the pursuit of a life rooted and grounded in God.

> *A revelation of who you are and whose you are releases a breakthrough of power and purpose in your life.*

All over the globe, regardless of age or ethnicity, people long for the love of a parent in their lives. Everyone wants to know that they are loved and accepted unconditionally. It is a great desire placed within each of us by a loving Father who created us. We were designed to crave parental guidance and nurturing. It is what ultimately leads us to the heart of the Father and the acceptance of His Son as Savior. God is so smart that He knew He had to place certain instincts within us to draw us to Himself. Otherwise, our adversary and the fallen human nature would lead us astray forever.

I wandered aimlessly for many years prior to knowing God as Father. I had to receive this truth by faith before I could accept it as a reality in my heart. No one has a perfect family life. Even those families that seem to be absolutely flawless from the outside have their own issues and troubled waters to navigate. Mothers and fathers have fallen short, as have children. Sin has infiltrated every life in one way or another. Satan has had his destructive claws in the family unit since the first family entered the Garden of Eden. Imperfect people in imperfect families have hurt those closest to them, often leaving lifelong scars. These scars are the reason that many of God's children refuse Him as Father. I have personally witnessed adults weeping like babies because of the absence or abuse of a father figure in their lives. People fall into deep dark sin and degrading occupations because they never received words of love and affirmation from a parent. Knowing God as Father and allowing *Him* to reveal your true identity is essential to being made whole. He is the One who gave you life, and He loves you more than you love yourself.

Jeremiah 1:5 says, "Before I formed you in the womb I knew you." Your Creator knew exactly which sperm needed to unite with exactly which egg to bring you into existence at exactly the right time. He has a perfect will and purpose for your life. His plans for you are bigger than you. He knew you before you were born. He knew you before you had an earthly mother or father. He knew *you* before you knew *Him*. He knew that you would be a mess at times. He knew that people would fail you often. He knew that you would suffer disappointment and heartache during your lifetime, even from the ones who call you their own. He knew that people would discard you and that Satan would lie to you. He knew all of this, and He chose to reveal Himself as Father for that very reason. *You need Him as Father.* We all do.

In Acts 17, Paul, Silas, Timothy, and others travelled through Thessalonica, Berea, and Athens preaching Jesus. They revealed true identity to those who would hear their messages. They spoke to Jews in the synagogues, to Gentile worshipers, and to people in the marketplace, teaching them about who God says they are. Upon noticing an altar with the inscription "TO THE UNKNOWN GOD," Paul seized his divine opportunity to make God "known." He spoke in the midst of the Areopagus, the highest judicial and legislative council of ancient Athens. He quoted their own poets, saying, "For we are also His offspring." Within the context of his teaching about the character and nature of God, Paul recognized the importance of sharing with them that they were born of the Father. This unknown god they worshiped could not give them what they deeply desired to have. Only a loving Creator who revealed Himself as Father could do that. Paul knew that what they ultimately wanted was to be in a family. They wanted what we all want: LOVE.

God sees all and knows all. We are not fooling Him with our masks and charades. He peers right through all of the ways we try to cover our pain, hide our heartache, and fill our voids. He stares straight into the hearts of His precious ones and knows the truth.

My parents divorced when I was nine years old. Their separation was a tremendous shock for me as a young girl, and the trauma of that event caused me to shut down in many ways. I lived with deep torment for over twenty years before I acknowledged that I needed help. I struggled with abandonment, rejection, and fear, but I tried to act like I had it all together. Life on the outside seemed great, but I was dying on the inside. In

> "Before I formed you in the womb I knew you."
>
> Jeremiah 1:5

my weakness, God began to reveal His strength.[45] Once I started reading my Bible, the Lord opened the eyes of my heart concerning His pure, perfect, parental love. He helped me forgive others and ask for their forgiveness as well. His love for me as a daughter satisfied one of the greatest longings of my heart, and I was finally free to love others as He has always loved me.

When you become a Christian, you step into a new family. Spiritual mothers, fathers, brothers, and sisters will gather around you through the blood of Jesus and the unity of the Spirit. God will fill every void and heal every hurt caused by the

---

[45]   2 Corinthians 12:9

shortcomings of your earthly family as you learn to trust Him and rely on Him as Father. Psalm 68:5 says that He is a "father of the fatherless." Do not pity your life or situation and do not let the enemy of your soul sabotage you with guilt, lies, shame, or confusion. You have a Father in heaven who adores you. He knows the number of hairs on your head and cares about every detail of your life.[46] He never leaves your side. He is perfect. There is no spot or blemish in Him. He *cannot* fail. He is faithful and true, and His love endures forever.

Regardless of where you are on your journey, God wants to meet you right now in a fresh way as Father. He wants to speak identity into your life, satisfy every need, protect and provide for you, and reveal His great love. He wants to welcome you into His family and watch you blossom and grow into the fullness of who *He* says you are. As you do, you will become a better parent, spouse, child, friend, and member of society. Knowing God as Father brings completion to your heart in a way that nothing else can.

We are living in an hour of history that requires us to have a great understanding of who we are as Christians. The darkness will continue to grow darker, which means the brightness within us must grow brighter. We must know what God says about us in John 1:12-13, "But as many as received Him, to them He gave the right to become children of God, to those who believe in His name: who were born, not of blood, nor of the will of the flesh, nor of the will of man, but of God." No one is truly fulfilled apart from the revelation of God as Father. He created us to know Him in that way. He revealed Himself as *Father* and sent His *Son* to die for the sins of His *offspring*. God has *family* on His mind.

> *Knowing God as Father brings completion to your heart in a way that nothing else can.*

In Acts 17:6, the disciples were referred to as those "who have turned the world upside down." This is the evidence of

---

46   Luke 12:7, Psalm 139

a life lived on purpose with a real understanding of *who* you are and *whose* you are. Once this is established in your heart, nothing will be impossible for you.[47] Accept your identity and inheritance as a child of God and ask Him to reveal the benefits of being called His offspring. He is a good Daddy, and you are His prized possession.

---

[47] Mark 9:23

Pause and Reflect

How does it make you feel to think about being the offspring of the Father of all creation? Are you able to relate to Him as His child? Why or why not?

_____

_____

_____

_____

_____

_____

_____

_____

_____

_____

Raw and Real

An incorrect perspective of God is keeping His children from knowing Him as Father.

Short and Sweet

Our Father in heaven, holy is Your Name. Thank You for calling me Your child. Reveal Yourself as Father and help me receive Your love in the areas where I have been wounded. Heal me and teach me how to forgive those who have hurt me. Amen.

Meditate and Memorize

"Therefore, since we are the offspring of God, we ought not to think that the Divine Nature is like gold or silver or stone, something shaped by art and man's devising."
—Acts 17:29

Believe and Receive

I am a child of God.

Listen and Learn
Get personal with your Father.

Create and Relate
Use this space to connect with God through creativity.

OCCUPATION

τέχνη

technē

tekh'-nay

art, craft;
a trade or skill

Your occupation is not merely something you "do." It corresponds with who you are. It identifies the particular season you are in with God, but it does not define you. Only your relationship with God should define you. However, your life's work plays an important role in establishing your identity as a child of God.

I have heard people say that we are human "BE"ings, not human "DO"ings, and to a certain extent that is correct. God longs to "BE" with His children. He wants to abide with us and have a relationship with us. The more time you spend with Him, the more you desire His presence. The more you encounter His beautiful nature, the more you want to *do* for Him. Out of that longing to *do* something for God—to give back to the Giver Himself—comes a realization that the work you do is not independent of your relationship with Him. God wants to partner with you in your occupation to bring His kingdom to earth.

I have had many jobs over the years, but I never truly knew what my life's calling was until I began to seek God about my identity. I had to ask the tough questions: "Who am I, Lord? Why am I here?" I had to do some deep digging into the soil of my own heart and discover my passions. I had to be still in His presence and listen to His voice as He revealed the truth about who *He* says I am. It is a process. The answers do not come all at once. This life is a marathon, not a sprint, and every step counts as you pursue your goal of finishing the race set before you.

> *God wants to partner with you in your occupation to bring His kingdom to earth.*

The world will lie to you. In fact, the father of lies (Satan) began relentlessly attacking your identity as soon as you entered this world. The prince of the air has been sabotaging your destiny through the radio, the television, the movie screen, the Internet, and other media outlets all of your life. Bullies in school called you names, authority figures crushed your hopes and dreams, and naysayers told you that "you can't" or "that's impossible." Skewed perceptions of identity have been infiltrating your mind, will, and emotions since the moment you were born, and your Father in heaven is ready to set the record straight.

All of these lies cause ungodly beliefs to take root in our lives. As a result, people are striving to become something or someone that a warped culture has convinced them they need to be. They are desperate for acceptance from friends, family, and society in general. They are searching for something that can only be found in God. God wants to heal the identity crisis that has caused His children to wander aimlessly in the wilderness for far too long.

Throughout my life, I have been a jack of all trades (and master of none). I bounced around for years searching for a "career" that would fit and fill me. I worked in retail, sales, service, management, . . . and the list goes on. I chased fleshly desires and climbed corporate ladders. Looking back, there was always something inside of me that said, "There is more." That small, still voice—some call it intuition—would never allow me to be perfectly content. God had a bigger plan. 1 Corinthians 2:9 says, "Eye has not seen, nor ear heard, nor have entered into the heart of man the things which God has prepared for those who love Him."

I floundered for a long time trying to figure out what I wanted to "do" with my life. I always felt like something was missing. And it was—a relationship with my Creator, the only One who knows me better than I know myself. No job or career, regardless of how exciting or lucrative it was, could satisfy the longing in my heart to be loved by God and live my life on purpose for His glory.

Your walk with God may lead you in and out of various vocations, as mine has. You may wait tables one year and start your own business the next. You may retire as a teacher then become a missionary. You may be a professional actor, athlete, or musician for a time then decide to use that platform to help impoverished people around the world. You may be a CEO in corporate America one moment and a politician the next. Nothing is wasted in the kingdom of God. If you navigate those transitions with His greater purpose in mind, you will maintain a clear perspective regarding the path He has chosen for you. Do not box yourself in or settle for less than God's best. Dream big and be a wise steward of everything He gave you. All of your desires, hopes, talents, and abilities are there for a reason.

The Apostle Paul was used in many different ways in the book of Acts. In Acts 18, he worked as a tentmaker, he reasoned with the Jews in the synagogues, he taught the word of God, he traveled to various locations to share the gospel, and he strengthened the disciples. He was a manual laborer, a preacher, a teacher, a missionary, and a pastor all in one chapter. Above all, he was a Spirit-filled follower of Christ who sought to live out his purpose on the earth one day at a time.

Jesus said, "My food is to do the will of Him who sent Me, and to finish His work."[48] The Greek word for *work* in that verse is *ergon* (see also Chapter 13, page 121). It refers to labor, toil, business, or employment. It is defined as "anything accomplished by hand, art, industry, or mind." The work God calls you to do will be exactly that . . . work. You cannot escape laboring for your reward, in the natural as well as in the spirit. The key to living a life of fulfillment and joy as you labor is to do what you have been created to do. Work wholeheartedly unto the Lord, using your gifts, skills, knowledge, and experience to make a difference in the world. Proverbs 16:3 says, "Commit your works to the Lord, and your thoughts will be established." The original Hebrew word for *works* in that verse actually translates as *labor* or *occupation*. The Bible instructs God's people to trust Him completely with their work, their labor, and their occupation. Only then will we truly succeed.

> *All of your desires, hopes, talents, and abilities are there for a reason.*

So what do you do when the bills need to be paid, there are mouths to feed, and you are stuck in a boring 9-5 job that you do not enjoy? First, you determine if that is where God has called you to be. If it is, then you commit your work to the Lord, laboring joyfully and diligently as your service unto Him. If it is not, then you spend time in prayer, seek wise

---

[48] John 4:34

counsel, and follow the voice of the Holy Spirit. His leadership is perfect. Isaiah 30:21 reminds us that "Your ears shall hear a word behind you, saying, 'This is the way, walk in it.'" The Holy Spirit's job is to guide you into all truth.[49] He is your helper, counselor, and advocate.[50] As you follow Him and submit to His wisdom, doors of opportunity will open, and you will be ushered into your destiny one step at a time.

Your occupation is a means to an end. It is your livelihood, an avenue for provision in your life. On a broader scale, the work you do is intended to help you reach souls for Christ and make a difference in the lives of those with whom you come in contact. It is one of your spheres of influence. Think of it as the territory God has given you to conquer and claim for His kingdom. This is accomplished through your faithfulness, prayers, testimony, and witness. You are expected to exemplify the character and nature of Christ everywhere you go. Therefore, your job is also your mission field.

The word of God has much to say regarding work. In 1 Thessalonians 4:10-11, Paul writes, "But we urge you, brethren, that you increase more and more; that you also aspire to lead a quiet life, to mind your own business, and to work with your own hands, as we commanded you, that you may walk properly toward those who are outside, and that you may lack nothing." Again in 2 Thessalonians 3:10, Paul issues a reminder, "If anyone will not work, neither shall he eat." Throughout His word, God promises to bless the work of our hands. It is important to note, however, that we can do work that pleases God or we can do work that provokes Him to anger.[51] Think about that for a moment. Does your work please the Lord? Is He blessing it?

Proverbs 23:4-5 admonishes, "Do not overwork to be rich . . . For riches certainly make themselves wings; they fly away like an eagle toward heaven." In Matthew 6:19-21, Jesus instructs, "Do not lay up for yourselves treasures on earth, where moth and rust destroy and where thieves break in and steal; but lay up for yourselves treasures in heaven, where neither moth nor

---

[49]   John 16:13
[50]   John 14:15-18
[51]   Deuteronomy 31:29

rust destroys and where thieves do not break in and steal. For where your treasure is, there your heart will be also."

Are you overworking? If so, what is your motivation? Where are you storing your treasures? In houses built by man or in heaven where there is an eternal reward for your labor? Are you resting and honoring the Sabbath as the Lord commands? According to the account of creation in Genesis, God Himself worked faithfully for six days creating the heavens and the earth and everything in them. Then He rested. *God works. God rests.* This is the pattern He established for His children at the beginning of time, and it continues to this day. He promises blessings for obedience.[52]

What is your craft? Where are you gifted? What skills have you acquired? What are you passionate about? What makes you come alive? What is it that you would do for free because you love it so much? God does not want you to be depressed and despondent in your occupation. Imagine what Paul's journey would have been like if he was bitter and resentful every step of the way. Instead, his passion and his purpose inspired him to do the work that he did in the book of Acts. As a result, lives are still being changed today.

Paul's experience on the road to Damascus confirmed what he was created to do. One life-changing encounter with Jesus solidified his destiny. From that moment forward, Paul lived with intention. He allowed every aspect of his life to glorify God. There is eternal joy in that place. There is an ability to sing songs even when in prison. There is a willingness to pay any price to fulfill God's divinely orchestrated plans for your life. There is a heartfelt desire to follow Him daily. There is something inside of you that rises up and says, *"I was created for this, and I will NEVER give up!"* This was the life of Paul in Acts 18.

> *You will stand before God one glorious day and give an account for the way you used what He gave you.*

---

[52] Deuteronomy 28

You will stand before God one glorious day and give an account for the way you used what He gave you. Do not live without purpose or passion and do not bury your talents. I cannot assure you that every day will be easy as you pursue the call of God on your life, but I can guarantee that it will be worth it. God wants to be known by ALL, and the ALL can only be reached as Christians step into their God-ordained destinies and do what they were created to do.

There is always risk involved when you are growing and advancing in the kingdom of God. You will be stretched beyond your comfort zone. If you do not believe me, look at Paul. However, with great risk comes great reward. Life is too short to live without passion and purpose for the glory of God. Use wisdom and discernment, seek counsel when necessary, and always follow the leadership of the Holy Spirit as you pursue His plans for your life. Let the light of the Lord shine through you while you work joyfully, diligently, and with excellence unto Him. And remember this: When it comes to your occupation, do what you love, and love what you do!

Pause and Reflect
Are you living purposefully and passionately? Are you doing the work God created you to do? Why or why not?

_____

_____

_____

_____

_____

_____

_____

_____

_____

_____

_____

_____

Raw and Real
Too many Christians are miserable in their occupations and never truly experience a life lived on purpose.

Short and Sweet
Creator God, Your plan for my life is perfect. Help me live and work according to your perfect will and for Your glory. Holy Spirit, lead me and guide me into all truth as I continue to discover who I am in You. Amen.

Meditate and Memorize
"So, because he was of the same trade, he stayed with them and worked; for by occupation they were tentmakers."
—Acts 18:3

Believe and Receive
God blesses the work of my hands.

Listen and Learn

Talk to God about your occupation.

_____
_____
_____
_____
_____
_____
_____
_____
_____
_____
_____
_____
_____
_____
_____
_____
_____
_____
_____
_____
_____
_____
_____
_____
_____
_____
_____
_____
_____
_____
_____
_____
_____
_____
_____

Create and Relate
Use this space to connect with God through creativity.

ACTS 19
DAY NINETEEN

MIRACLES

δύναμις

dunamis

doo'-nam-is

wonderful work;
ability, abundance;
might, strength, violence;
inherent force or power

Acts 19 ranks as one of my favorite chapters in the Bible. Since I began to study the word of God as a new Christian, this chapter has moved me in ways I cannot explain. It is filled with truth and the supernatural power of a miracle-working God. It reminds me, each time I read it, that He wants to use His children to reveal Himself in mighty ways.

It is interesting to note that the Greek word translated as *miracles* in this chapter is *dunamis*. This is the same word that is used when referring to God's *power* in verses such as Acts 1:8, "But you shall receive power when the Holy Spirit has come upon you; and you shall be witnesses to Me in Jerusalem, and in all Judea and Samaria, and to the end of the earth." It is also used in Acts 10:38, "God anointed Jesus of Nazareth with the Holy Spirit and with power, who went about doing good and healing all who were oppressed by the devil, for God was with Him." This miraculous power is available to every believer today.

The *dunamis power* of God is explosive, hence the origin of the English word *dynamite*. This is the power that Jesus exhibited on a daily basis as He healed the sick, raised the dead, cast out demons, calmed the seas, and preached the gospel. After His resurrection, Jesus sent His Spirit to empower His followers to do even greater works than He did. Do you understand that you have access to the same power that Jesus had? Think about that for a moment. Does your life reflect His wonder-working power? I have a friend who recently reminded me, "Life is boring without it."

> *Do you understand that you have access to the same power that Jesus had?*

Acts 19 needs to be studied in order to better understand the power of God as it applies to all born-again, Spirit-filled Christians. When I first became interested in the miracles of the Bible, God warned me, "Never forget the miracle of the transformed human heart." This, in my opinion, is one of the greatest evidences of the power of God at work on the earth today. When a stony, stubborn heart is turned to soft, pliable flesh for the glory of God, it is a miracle indeed.[53] When a sinful, rebellious creature is miraculously converted into a gentle, loving servant, there is no better testimony of the supernatural power of a loving God.

As we read through the book of Acts, we become modern-day witnesses of everything the disciples said and did as God used them to perform miracles. This great book is intended to encourage us that God will use us in the very same way. Christianity is not about going to church once or twice each week and saying your prayers every night before you go to sleep. There is so much more to this life we have in Christ. God wants to *know* you. He wants to be *known* by you. He wants to walk in intimacy with you as His beloved child and friend. John 15:15 says, "No longer do I call you servants, for a servant does not know what his master is doing; but I have called you friends, for all things that I heard from My Father I have made known to you." God wants to partner with you to reveal His love and power to a lost and dying world.

Every child carries the DNA of his or her father. Your Father in heaven wants to help you understand the *dunamis power* that resides in your spiritual DNA. You are the offspring of the Creator of the universe. He is the One who spoke everything into existence from nothing. He is the One who raised Jesus, Lazarus, Tabitha, Eutychus (and many others) from the dead. He wants to be known in that way by all who call themselves His followers. I believe this is one of the most overlooked and neglected aspects of the nature of God in the Body of Christ today. Christ calls us His Body because He longs to be *deeply connected* to each and every member. He reveals Himself as Bridegroom because He is seeking a *loving relationship* with His Bride. God wants to teach you about Himself as you allow His Spirit to flow through you. He wants to partner with you in intimacy to release His power on the earth. Jeremiah 33:3 says, "Call to Me, and I will answer you, and show you great and mighty things, which you do not know." When God answers, miracles happen.

---

[53] Ezekiel 11:19-20

Several miracles occur in this chapter. They all deserve attention, but we will focus on a few of them here. The first notable miracle in Acts 19 is the baptism of the Holy Spirit. Think about this with me for a moment. Paul specifically referred to two separate baptisms in this passage of Scripture. He was having a conversation with some believers in Ephesus, and he asked them, "Did you receive the Holy Spirit when you believed?"[54] They were completely unaware that the Holy Spirit existed and replied that they had only been baptized with John's baptism of repentance (water baptism). Paul explained that Jesus came to baptize with the Holy Spirit so that all believers could experience the miraculous power and indwelling presence of God.[55] Upon believing and receiving this glorious truth, Acts 19:6 says, "And when Paul had laid hands on them, the Holy Spirit came upon them, and they spoke with tongues and prophesied." Talk about a miracle!

> *Your Father in heaven wants to help you understand the dunamis power that resides in your spiritual DNA.*

The baptism of the Holy Spirit with the evidence of tongues and prophecy is one of the most critical components of the Christian life. It is also one of the most controversial. It is this very baptism, however, that causes the Christian to know God in a way that He cannot otherwise be known. The Spirit of the living God chooses to dwell within the mortal body of a believer. This is a miracle that the finite human mind cannot fathom. Fortunately, God has elected to bypass mankind's natural intellect in order to reveal His true *super*natural nature through the indwelling presence of His Spirit.

God is inexhaustible. There is always more of Him to experience and encounter. You must not allow a fear of man or a fear of the unknown to keep you from His best. Everything about God is controversial in a world controlled and

---

[54] Acts 19:2

[55] Matthew 3:11

manipulated by Satan, the father of all lies.[56] As Christians, we must know and believe that God is good all the time. Even in the midst of a lack of understanding, we must remember that God is a *good* Father who delights in giving *good* gifts to His children.[57] In Matthew 7:11, Jesus said, "If you then, being evil, know how to give good gifts to your children, how much more will your Father who is in heaven give good things to those who ask Him!" This includes the blessings of tongues and prophecy that are available to *all* through the baptism of the Holy Spirit.

"Tongues" is a miracle of supernatural language that enables a believer to communicate with God beyond mental comprehension and understanding. The Apostle Paul said, "I thank my God I speak with tongues more than you all."[58] When you "speak in tongues" or "pray in the spirit," you are being strengthened from the inside out. You are also communicating directly with God about things that you may not otherwise be able to verbalize or express.[59] This is one of the miraculous ways God has chosen to edify believers through His Spirit. It fosters intimacy with Him and empowers us to do all that He has called and chosen us to do.

Many leaders in the Body of Christ do not discuss the importance of this heavenly prayer language. For countless Christians and denominations, the subject is taboo. Early in my walk with God, I began to seek truth in His word with a passion that could not be quenched. Less than eighteen months after my water baptism, I received the baptism "with the Holy Spirit and fire" that John the Baptist spoke of in Luke 3:16. I received "the Promise of the Father" that Jesus commanded His disciples to wait for in Acts 1:5, ". . . for John truly baptized with water, but you shall be baptized with the Holy Spirit not many days from now." I began to speak with tongues and prophesy, just as the disciples did in Acts. My life has been exponentially empowered as a result of the presence of the Holy Spirit. Prior to this baptism, I would pray for hours each day in my native language,

---

[56] John 8:44
[57] James 1:17
[58] 1 Corinthians 14:18
[59] 1 Corinthians 14:2

but I was frustrated because I could not break through in my prayer life. This all changed when I began to speak in tongues. Now I literally feel His fiery presence burning within me on a daily basis. I thank God for His Holy Spirit!

Another miraculous evidence of the Holy Spirit experienced by the believers in Acts 19 is that of prophecy. The *Enhanced Strong's Dictionary* (used by Olive Tree Bible Software) defines prophecy as a "discourse emanating from divine inspiration and declaring the purposes of God, whether by reproving and admonishing the wicked, or comforting the afflicted, or revealing things hidden; especially by foretelling future events." According to Revelation 19:10, "For the testimony of Jesus is the spirit of prophecy." The Spirit of Truth knows *all* things about *all* people at *all* times. His prophetic words spoken through a believer offer powerful opportunities to reveal Christ to others.

Tongues and prophecy are miraculous manifestations of the supernatural power of God. They are freely given to all who willingly seek and accept His presence and truth. Many people read the book of Acts and believe that God stopped working miracles two thousand years ago. Generally speaking, however, miracles occur all around us on a daily basis. They vary in size and scope—from raising the dead to finding a $20 bill in your pocket. You experience a miracle every day when you wake up with breath in your lungs. God sustains our lives by miraculously holding *all* things together—inside and out. Consider the suspension of earth in the vast expanse of the universe and the phenomenal inner workings of the human body. Imagine the sun majestically rising over the ocean or a glistening rainbow appearing on a cloudy day. Contemplate the acorn's progression into a mighty oak and the forming of a tiny frame in a mother's womb. These are all powerful reminders that God is still working miracles today.

God sustains our lives by miraculously holding all things together—inside and out.

Acts 19:11-12 says, "Now God worked unusual miracles by the hands of Paul, so that even handkerchiefs or aprons were brought from his body to the sick, and the diseases left them and the evil spirits went out of them." *Unusual* miracles indeed! It is important to note that the seven sons of Sceva, along with some Jewish exorcists, attempted to cast out evil spirits as Paul did. However, they did not know Jesus Christ as their personal Lord and Savior. Acts 19:15 says, "And the evil spirit answered and said, 'Jesus I know, and Paul I know; but who are you?'" Do not make the same mistake that these unbelieving men made. Evil spirits will recognize, resist, and prevail against those who have selfish or impure motives. The power of God is not to be abused by people seeking to exalt themselves. God will not permit the name of Jesus to be prostituted for man's glory. He wants to use you to perform unusual miracles, signs, and wonders, but He will only allow His power to flow through those who truly *know* Him.

God shows no partiality.[60] He is simply looking for some radically faithful people who are hungry for more. He wants compassionate servants like Paul who will obey His voice and follow Him wholeheartedly. Pockets of His powerful presence are springing up around the globe. This is His desire for *all* who believe. He wants to encounter you and use you in earth-shaking ways. Do not be like the seven sons of Sceva and attempt to seek His power apart from intimacy. Rather, seek His face and search His heart with a deep longing to *know* Him in every way. Then expect Him to use you miraculously like He used Paul in Acts 19.

---

[60] Acts 10:34

Pause and Reflect

Have you received the baptism of the Holy Spirit? How do you know if you have or have not? Do you believe miracles still occur today?

_____

_____

_____

_____

_____

_____

_____

_____

_____

_____

Raw and Real

God wants to ignite His church with miracles and power, but people are too complacent in watered-down Christianity to catch fire.

Short and Sweet

Powerful and Miraculous Creator, You alone are able to do the impossible. Heal my unbelief, purify my heart, and reveal Your truth to me today. Use me for Your glory. Amen.

Meditate and Memorize

"Now God worked unusual miracles by the hands of Paul, so that even handkerchiefs or aprons were brought from his body to the sick, and the diseases left them and the evil spirits went out of them."
—Acts 19:11-12

Believe and Receive

Miracles are real.

Listen and Learn

Ask God to increase your faith for miracles.

_____

_____

_____

_____

_____

_____

_____

_____

_____

_____

_____

_____

_____

_____

_____

_____

_____

_____

_____

_____

_____

_____

_____

_____

_____

_____

_____

_____

_____

_____

_____

_____

_____

Create and Relate
Use this space to connect with God through creativity.

ACTS 20
DAY TWENTY

PURCHASED

περιποιέομαι

peripoieomai

per-ee-poy-eh'-om-ahee

to acquire or buy;
to reserve or keep safe;
to preserve for one's self

Acts 20:28 says, "Therefore take heed to yourselves and to all the flock, among which the Holy Spirit has made you overseers, to shepherd the church of God which He purchased with His own blood." Why did Paul use the word *purchased* in that scripture? What does it mean and how does it affect us individually and corporately? This is a concept that must be grasped as we pursue greater intimacy with God and a better understanding of who He has called us to be. Apart from the revelation of being purchased by a holy God, it is impossible to grow in the knowledge of who Jesus is and what He did for each and every one of us on that cross two millennia ago.

So how did His blood purchase us? How is that even possible? When I think of someone being purchased, it brings up uncomfortable images of slavery. It reminds me that an actual price was placed on the life of an individual who was then used for the benefit of another. How can we know that being purchased by God is different from being purchased by man? Let us take a deeper look at this word as it relates to the price Jesus paid for all and study the impact it has on the identity of a Christian.

The Bible tells us in Leviticus 17:11, "For the life of the flesh is in the blood, and I have given it to you upon the altar to make atonement for your souls; for it is the blood that makes atonement for the soul." Have you ever wondered why *blood* is so important to God? And how does it make "atonement" for our souls?

The shedding of blood for the sins of man dates back to the Garden of Eden. In Genesis 3:21, God covered Adam and Eve with the skin of an animal after they had sinned—indicating that blood was shed for them. Later on, the Israelites made offerings that required a blood sacrifice as payment for sin.

In the Old Testament, under the old covenant, an animal was killed, and the blood of that animal was used to "cover" the sins of God's people. In other words, the sins were still there, they were just "hidden" from God's sight and not held against the sinner.

The penalty for sin is, and always has been, death. Genesis 2:16-17 says, "And the Lord God commanded the man, saying, 'Of every tree of the garden you may freely eat; but of the tree of the knowledge of good and evil you shall not eat, for in the day that you eat of it you shall surely die.'" Paul confirms this in Romans 6:23, "For the wages of sin is death, but the gift of God is eternal life in Christ Jesus our Lord." Sin yields death. Period. It is clear then that this is not only a matter of sin; it is also a matter of life versus death. This is where the blood comes in.

Consider that blood is the carrier of *life*. It is the fluid that delivers necessary nutrients and oxygen to the cells of the body, while transporting waste away from those same cells. Blood is also used to determine ancestry. Your earthly identity is stored in your blood through strands of DNA located in your cells. Your genealogy and your physical appearance can both be determined through a sample of your blood. Blood is the life force that sustains humanity. It connects us as family and keeps us alive in every sense of the word. Without blood, our human bodies would die.

Do you understand why part of the Levitical law forbade the drinking of blood or eating of meat with its blood still intact? It is because the *life* of the flesh, as Leviticus 17:11 tells us, is definitely found in the blood. All of the Old Testament shedding of blood symbolically foreshadowed the life and death of Christ. God sent His only Son to die for our sins by shedding His perfect and holy blood on the cross. He could have chosen any method of redemption, but He chose the outpouring of blood. God chose to cleanse us with His very own *life* force. He chose to purchase us with the sacrifice of Himself. Romans 5:8-9 says, "But God demonstrates His own love toward us, in that while we were still sinners, Christ died for us. Much more then, having now

> *Your earthly identity is stored in your blood through strands of DNA located in your cells.*

been justified by His blood, we shall be saved from wrath through Him."

During the first Passover in Exodus 12, the blood of an unblemished lamb was placed on the doorpost of every Israelite's home, symbolizing covering and protection from death. Exodus 12:13 says, "Now the blood shall be a sign for you on the houses where you are. And when I see the blood, I will pass over you; and the plague shall not be on you to destroy you when I strike the land of Egypt." It was this blood that freed the Israelites from 400 years of slavery in Egypt. The reason you and I are not required to sacrifice animals as reparation for our sins today is because one Spotless Lamb (Jesus), without sin or blemish, died on a cross and paid the price for our forgiveness. He redeemed us; He *purchased* us. Holy, Holy, Holy is He!

In the Old Testament, the grace of God provided a substitutionary atonement for sin through the spilled blood of an animal. The Hebrew word for *atonement* in the Old Testament *(kâphar)* means "to cover." In the New Testament, the Greek word for *atonement (katallagē)* means "reconciliation." In the New Testament, sin was no longer simply *covered*. Instead, the blood of Jesus completely washed it away! Hallelujah!

The shed blood of Jesus became the connective tissue that unites God's children and grafts them into His family. The blood of Christ deposits the DNA of the heavenly Father into the life of every believer. We take on His divine characteristics and His identity in place of our fleshly nature. 1 John 2:2 says, "And He Himself is the propitiation for our sins, and not for ours only but also for the whole world." *Strong's Complete Word Study Concordance* defines *propitiation* as "that which appeases anger and brings reconciliation with someone who has reason to be angry." Through the shedding of His blood, Jesus appeased the wrath of God and *became* the atoning sacrifice for all of mankind. Think of it this way, Christ's ATONEment made us "AT ONE" with a righteous, holy God.

The blood of Jesus is often referred to as *the scarlet thread of redemption* that is woven throughout the word of God, linking the Old and New Testaments. Ephesians 1:7 says, "In Him we have redemption through His blood, the forgiveness of sins, according to the riches of His grace . . . ." Redemption is a word with its origins in the slave market. The premise is that a person is released from bondage through the payment of a ransom. To *redeem* literally means *to purchase back from slavery.* Jesus essentially went into the slave market of sin and purchased freedom for the sinner with His blood. John 8:34-36 says, ". . . whoever commits sin is a slave of sin. And a slave does not abide in the house forever, but a son abides forever. Therefore if the Son makes you free, you shall be free indeed." You were a slave to sin, death, and evil, but the blood of Jesus purchased your freedom. Because of His blood, God sees you as a son or daughter of the Light and no longer as a slave to darkness.[61] Oh, the glorious liberty we have been granted because of the price He paid for our sins!

The blood of Christ purifies us. Hebrews 9:22 verifies this: "And according to the law almost all things are purified with blood, and without shedding of blood there is no remission." The word *remission* in that verse is the Greek word *aphesis.* It refers to a release from bondage or imprisonment. It implies deliverance, forgiveness, or pardon of sins—letting them go as if they had never been committed.

> *Jesus essentially went into the slave market of sin and purchased freedom for the sinner with His blood.*

Isaiah 1:18 says, "Though your sins are like scarlet, they shall be as white as snow; though they are red like crimson, they shall be as wool."

There is no amount of money on the face of the earth that could have purchased your freedom. A sacrifice had to be made for the forgiveness of your sins—to spare you from the penalty of death. Not just any sacrifice, but the selfless and perfect sacrifice of the only begotten Son of God. The price that was paid for you through the shed blood of Christ allows you to stand

---

[61]   Galatians 4:7

in the presence of your holy heavenly Father and commune with Him. He sees you through the blood of Jesus, and He calls you righteous. This is a concept that is too great and too beautiful for the human mind to fathom. It will never be comprehended completely this side of heaven. Blood redemption is much more complex than any commentary or Bible study could adequately explain. We may experience a bit of the glory that accompanies the revelation of the crucifixion of Christ, but the fullness of that purchase is yet to be received.

Paul deemed this topic important enough to discuss during his final exhortation to the elders of the church of Ephesus in Acts 20. He reminded them that the church of God had been purchased with the blood of Christ. What has His blood purchased for *you* personally as a member of the family of God? Because of the blood of Jesus, you have entered into a new covenant relationship with God (Luke 22:20). You have been justified and delivered from the wrath of God (Romans 5:9). You have the opportunity to draw near to God (Ephesians 2:13) and the ability to enjoy peace with God (Colossians 1:20). You have been granted the boldness and authority to enter God's holy presence (Hebrews 10:19), and you can experience the delight of victory as an overcomer of evil (Revelation 12:10-11).

In His final moments on the cross, Jesus declared, "It is finished!" That phrase is translated from the Greek word *tetelestai*, which means that something has been completed, perfected, and accomplished. The word *tetelestai* was also written on receipts in New Testament times indicating that a bill had been paid in full. This is what the blood of Jesus did for you. It discharged every debt and stamped "PAID IN FULL" across the sin and disobedience of your life. The finished work of Christ allows you to approach God without any sense of guilt, shame, or condemnation. *Tetelestai* is also a word used by artists and builders as they gaze upon their creations and note that there is nothing more that can be added. In other words, "This is complete. I have done everything according to plan."

Upon seeing Jesus, John the Baptist exclaimed, "Behold! The Lamb of God who takes away the sin of the world!"[62] It was the blood of the Lamb of God that saved your soul from death two thousand years ago, and it is still His precious blood that sets the captives free today. Thank Him for redeeming you from slavery by purchasing your freedom through the ultimate sacrifice of His life. The most beautiful person who ever lived gave Himself for you so you can know what He knows. God determined that no price was too high to have you near Him. As Jesus stretched His arms out on the cross on that fateful day, He was saying, "I love you this much."

> *God determined that no price was too high to have you near Him.*

---

[62] John 1:29

Pause and Reflect

Do you have a better understanding of what it means to be purchased by God? How will this affect your relationship with Him?

_____

_____

_____

_____

_____

_____

_____

_____

_____

_____

Raw and Real

Followers of Christ are no longer for sale.

Short and Sweet

Loving Savior and Redeemer, thank You for the price You paid for my freedom. Give me greater revelation concerning the power that lies in Your blood. Help me never forget that I have been eternally purchased by You. Amen.

Meditate and Memorize

"Therefore take heed to yourselves and to all the flock, among which the Holy Spirit has made you overseers, to shepherd the church of God which He purchased with His own blood."
—Acts 20:28

Believe and Receive

Jesus died for *me*.

Listen and Learn
Meditate on the Lamb of God.

Create and Relate

Use this space to connect with God through creativity.

ACTS 21
DAY TWENTY-ONE

DISCIPLE

μαθητής

mathētēs

math-ay-tes'

a learner or pupil

There are 27 specific references to "disciples" in the book of Acts, three of them being found in Acts 21. *Disciple* is both a noun and a verb. As a noun, it describes someone who is an avid student. As a verb, it is the act of teaching others what you have learned. Both are necessary components of being followers of Christ. The book of Acts gives us insight into the lives of the early disciples, and it teaches us how to become the church of Acts 29 by truly displaying the heart and actions of Christ.

When Jesus called the first disciples, He said, "Follow Me."[63] He was not only inviting them to physically walk where He walked, but He was also extending the unique opportunity to do what He did, say what He said, and feel what He felt. He was welcoming them into a personal relationship with Him through discipleship. He wanted to establish their identity by teaching them His ways and sending them out to do the same for others. How does this concept of discipleship apply to us today, two thousand years after the resurrection of Christ?

Let us recount some of the characteristics of the disciples in the Gospels as they literally lived in the presence of God. First of all, and most importantly, true followers and students of Christ wholeheartedly *believed* in Him. They also *followed* Him, *came* to Him, *spoke* to Him, *inquired* of Him, and *listened* to Him. They *answered* His call, *gathered* around Him, *drew near* to Him, and *relied* on Him.

> When Jesus called the first disciples, He said, "Follow Me."

They were *trained, equipped, instructed,* and *prepared* by Him. They *learned* from Him, were *empowered* by Him, *worked* with Him, and *obeyed* His commands. They were *loved, served, encouraged, comforted, forgiven, healed,* and *delivered* by Him. They *sought His help* in desperation and *endured suffering and persecution* for His name. They were *warned* by Him, *rebuked and disciplined* by Him, *challenged* by Him, and *offended* by Him. They *fellowshipped* with Him, *withdrew* with Him, and were *sent out*

---

[63] Matthew 4:19

by Him. In essence, His teaching and His presence *consumed* their entire lives. Oh, the wondrous pleasure of being able to experience Jesus in that way!

As we see in Acts 21, disciples were not only the twelve men called by Jesus at the beginning of His ministry. They were also countless other believers who chose to follow Him long after His resurrection. Disciples did not disappear after Jesus died; rather they have multiplied exponentially, filling the earth with the glory of God as carriers of His holy presence. Disciples are people who believe in the risen Lord and determine to live a life that exemplifies His character and nature.

After the ascension of Christ, with the help and empowerment of His Spirit, the disciples in the book of Acts began to take on new roles as ones who would go forth and do the greater works of which Jesus spoke.[64] They no longer had access to God in the flesh. Instead, they became totally reliant on his indwelling Spirit to teach, lead, and guide them. They also depended on one another for instruction and direction. They had been taught, and now it was time to teach.

We can learn a lot about the lifestyle of a modern-day disciple from The Acts of the Apostles. Acts 6:7 says, "Then the word of God spread, and the number of the disciples multiplied greatly . . . ." It is important to note that the disciples were continually increasing in number. As a result of that multiplication, there were more people available to do the work that God had called them to do, individually and corporately. They provided housing for those in need and sent relief to the brethren and elders. They strengthened, exhorted, encouraged, and supported each other. They gathered to break bread and spent time together as a family of believers. They worshipped, prayed, and fasted together. They performed miracles, signs, and wonders. They experienced blessing and conflict. They encountered trials and were threatened for their beliefs. Many of them faced death because of their relentless commitment to Christ. In the midst of all of that activity, Acts 13:52 says, "And the disciples were filled with joy and with the Holy Spirit."

---

[64] John 14:12

The life of a disciple is far from comfortable or complacent. It is an adventure like no other that is birthed out of a radical passion to serve the One who calls you His own. Are you following Christ as the disciples in Acts did? This may or may not mean that you travel the globe like Paul. Perhaps you are one of the disciples who will provide housing for a weary missionary or reach the lost in the marketplace. In His final commission, Jesus instructed His followers, "Go therefore and make disciples of all the nations, baptizing them in the name of the Father and of the Son and of the Holy Spirit, teaching them to observe all things that I have commanded you; and lo, I am with you always, even to the end of the age."[65] This command to make disciples still stands today. It is established first in your own heart, as you become a devoted disciple of Christ; then it is your duty to share Him with a desperately seeking world.

In my experience as a Christian, it has not been easy to find people who truly desire to disciple others. I have seen that zeal in corporate settings, but not as much on an individual basis. This has been frustrating for me at times. Our culture is permeated by such a "What's in it for me?" perspective that this often prevents the pure selfless love of Christ from freely flowing through us. Relationships take time to build, and most of us are simply too preoccupied with our own agendas to be available to build that intimacy with someone else. To be frank, people generally do not *want* to set aside their own agendas; they do not *want* to invest the time or energy; and they do not *care* that people are going to hell. It is sad, but true—selfishness and total indifference have invaded our hearts and lives.

> "Freely you have received, freely give."
>
> Matthew 10:8

Practically speaking, discipleship requires intention. It takes a focused effort to speak into someone else's life, teach and train them, and share your wisdom and experience. "Making

---

[65] Matthew 28:19-20

disciples" requires a long-term, willing commitment to see others succeed and excel, even beyond your own capacity or hope for their lives. As followers of Christ, it is our great privilege to lead people into a closer walk with Him. Helping others mature as Christians is an act of service unto the Lord.

I want to see people taking more of an initiative in the Body of Christ to seek out those who desire to grow in their knowledge and relationship with God. In Matthew 10:8, Jesus said, "Freely you have received, freely give." *You have so much to give.* Ask Him whom He wants you to pour your life and testimony into. Your life experience has prepared you to uniquely help others. Someone is hungry and thirsty today, and you possess the sustenance they need.

In Acts 19:1 and 21:4, we witness Paul "finding disciples" on his missionary journey, first at Ephesus, then again at Tyre. In Ephesus, he laid hands on them and baptized them with the Holy Spirit. In Tyre, they accompanied him with their wives and children, praying with him, until he was out of the city. Whether searching them out intentionally or meeting them unexpectedly, Paul regularly found himself in the company of other believers who supported his work, followed his teachings, and ultimately needed what God had placed inside of him. If Jesus showed up in your town today, would He find you as a disciple who is helping a brother or sister in need? Would He find you doing His work and leading others into a greater understanding of the truth?

Discipleship flows from a heart of abandoned love for the One who rescued you from sin and gave you the gift of eternal life. Every disciple has a teacher. The Holy Spirit is the greatest Teacher available to Christians today, but God also uses His earthen vessels to teach and lead people into the fullness of who He created

> *Being a disciple presents a lifelong opportunity to grow in the knowledge of who God is.*

them to be. Followers of Christ are commanded to walk in His ways and to teach others how to do the same. This is one of the greatest honors bestowed on believers and one that should be embraced on a daily basis.

Being a disciple presents a lifelong opportunity to grow in the knowledge of who God is. It enables you to become more like Him through the establishment of an intimate relationship with the great Rabbi and Teacher, Yeshua Jesus.

God is looking for willing ones. He will not force you to follow Him. He will gently welcome you into His presence and touch you so deeply that you consistently long for more of Him. Then He will send you out as an ambassador for His glory and give you a desire to teach others everything you have been taught.

Pause and Reflect
How does your life reflect your calling as a disciple? How will you make an effort to disciple others according to God's word?

_____
_____
_____
_____
_____
_____
_____
_____
_____
_____
_____
_____

Raw and Real
There is a big difference between being a fan of Christ and being a follower.

Short and Sweet
Faithful Teacher, I long to know more about You. Enable me to follow You with clean hands and a pure heart. Mold me, shape me, use me, send me, and train me in the way I should go. Help me disciple others according to Your word. Amen.

Meditate and Memorize
"Also some of the disciples from Caesarea went with us and brought with them a certain Mnason of Cyprus, an early disciple with whom we were to lodge."
—Acts 21:16

Believe and Receive
I am a disciple of Christ.

Listen and Learn
Ask the Holy Spirit to teach you something today.

Create and Relate
Use this space to connect with God through creativity.

TESTIMONY

μαρτυρια

marturia

mar-too-ree'-ah

evidence given;
record, report, witness

Every born again Christian possesses a testimony that encapsulates the power and goodness of God revealed through the shed blood of Jesus Christ. Apart from these elements, there is no authentic report of a salvation experience or life-altering encounter with God. Whether you were eight years old or eighty when you first received Him into Your heart, the gospel message is intricately woven into your story. As a believer, you have a testimony of the reality of a personal, loving God.

You may already know that you cannot have a *testi*mony without a *test*. Tests will occur strategically and consistently throughout your life. The purpose is to stretch you and increase your capacity to receive more of God. A newfound understanding of who God is will come from each season of adversity. Every trial will reveal His great love in a fresh way. Nothing is wasted in the kingdom of God. Genesis 50:20 says, "But as for you, you meant evil against me; but God meant it for good, in order to bring it about as it is this day, to save many people alive." Everything the enemy meant for your harm will be used to glorify God and save souls as you share your testimony with others.

Regarding tests, notice that when a student is taking a test, the teacher is silent. Why? Because the test reveals what the student has learned from the teacher. During a test, the teacher trusts that the student has done the necessary preparation to pass with excellence. In life, sometimes we ace our tests, sometimes we barely squeak by, and sometimes we bomb. God does not want us to fail. He gives us everything we will ever need to pass every test we will ever take, yet there are definitely times when the Teacher is silent. If He gave us all of the answers in the midst of our crises, we would never mature or advance in our faith. Nobody wants to remain in kindergarten forever, do they?

Nothing is wasted in the kingdom of God.

Every Christian is either going through a test, is in the middle of one, or is coming out of one. The good news is that there are endless opportunities to grow in your walk with God. As you lean into Him in the midst of pain, discomfort, and lack of understanding, you are allowing Him to prepare you for something greater. With every victory, you are better equipped to help someone else. As you pursue His word and His heart in your greatest times of need, you are being supernaturally positioned for promotion. As you humble yourself before His throne of grace, He will exalt you.

Trusting God is unfortunately not our first human response to tribulation. However, each time God proves Himself faithful, your confidence in Him increases. You also receive a new level of authority that enables you to help others who may be experiencing similar battles. This is how your personal testimony is developed.

Throughout our lives, we will inevitably face moments of decision where we can choose to rely upon God in troubled times or run from Him. I can personally testify that I slept with my proverbial running shoes on for many years, just in case something difficult transpired that I was incapable of handling. Because of a fear of abandonment that permeated my life at an early age, I was always afraid of being hurt. My response to that fear was to run from anything or anyone that had the potential to cause more pain in my life. I chose to "avoid" dealing with my own heart and issues by running away, rather than hitting my problems head on and seeking the help and healing that I needed.

I am thankful that God continues to use everything I have been through in my life in a very specific way. As I surrender to Him in a particular area, He begins the process of strengthening me and making me tenacious. Rather than taking the easy way out by "running" from a painful situation, I have learned to invite God into the middle of it. Instead of fighting in my flesh and looking for a quick fix, I have become more eager to learn the lesson God wants to teach me. Wrestling with God has produced a "never give up" attitude in my life that has helped me conquer obstacles intended to intimidate me.

Every time you wrestle with God, you will have a new victory to share with others. This adds another facet to the diamond of your life. It makes you shine more brilliantly and reflect His light more radiantly. Paul's life is a great example of this. While he shared his story with the violent mob in Jerusalem, he faced yet another test as the outraged Jews declared him unfit to live. He could choose to fight back with hatred or he could trust and rest in the God who promised him everlasting life and peace. Because of his faith, Paul was able to witness before an unruly crowd and boldly declare the goodness of God. He fearlessly proclaimed the truth regarding his encounter with Jesus on the road to Damascus. He allowed himself to be vulnerable as he relayed the humility he experienced through that encounter. He spoke of things that would easily offend the natural mind - such as seeing a bright light and hearing a voice from heaven - but he did so without concern, believing that it would bring glory to God. Paul's radical transformation ignited a fire within him that could not be quenched, even in the midst of life-threatening circumstances. All of these components combined to reveal the existence and reality of God in Paul's life.

We can learn a great deal from Paul's testimony in Acts 22. It provides an excellent outline regarding how to share your journey with others. For example, in the beginning Paul briefly discussed *who he was* and *from where he had come.* He *highlighted his upbringing and experience* in a way that was *relatable* to those who were listening. He *mentioned his past,* so the people could see that he had lived a very dark and destructive life before his encounter with Jesus. Then he told them exactly *where he was* and *what he was doing* when he met Jesus. He recounted those moments with emotion and humility, revealing the truth about the nature of God. He disclosed what was specifically said and done that caused him to live differently and with purpose. He concluded his discourse by divulging that God had given him very clear instructions regarding with whom he was to share his testimony.

> *The Holy Spirit will always lead you regarding what to share, when to share, and with whom to share.*

The Holy Spirit will always lead you regarding what to share, when to share, and with whom to share. Your testimony will become more complex as you grow and mature in your walk with God. Each time you pass a particular test, you add a new dimension to your story that enables you to relate to people with more compassion than before. For example, when you survive a life-threatening health condition, you can share your story with others who may be fighting a similar battle, giving them hope and encouragement. Sometimes our tests are physical, but they may also be emotional—such as the pain that accompanies divorce and loss. A test may be spiritual as well—for example, when your beliefs are being challenged or when you are questioning the love or existence of God. When you conquer each trial and struggle *by faith*, you gain a greater understanding of who God is and of who you are *in* Him.

A God who knows you better than you know yourself is weaving your personal tapestry moment by moment. With each encounter, He is revealing an aspect of His unending grace and goodness. It is the tough stuff that molds us and shapes us. We are continually being refined through challenging circumstances, battles, and hardships. James 1:2-4 says it best: "My brethren, count it all joy when you fall into various trials, knowing that the testing of your faith produces patience. But let patience have its perfect work, that you may be perfect and complete, lacking nothing."

After I surrendered my heart and life to Christ, I remember praying, "God, give me a testimony that touches the nations and changes the world for Your glory." In retrospect, I joke about how crazy that was. What was I thinking?! I initially thought that the majority of my testimony would involve the deliverance from sin and bondage that occurred when I made the decision to accept Christ. Although that is indeed part of it, I have discovered that I am a living example of how God continues to reveal Himself through tests and trials on a daily basis. I need God in *every* situation, *all* the time—good, bad, or indifferent.

Let's use this book as an example. It took me one year to write the manuscript for this study/devotional. From start to finish, it was a battle. Momma always said, "Nothing worth having comes easy." She was right! First, my grandmother passed away as soon as I began to write. Then I moved from the West Coast back home to the East Coast to be near my family. When I was four chapters away from completion, I dropped my laptop and lost *everything*! My manuscript was completely irretrievable (no, I did not have it backed up—I failed that test and had to take it over again). I truly felt like I had lost a baby. It was devastating. I had to muster the motivation to start over, trusting that this was God's plan and will, even when people suggested that I should "just give it up." Not long after that, the house I was living in was ransacked and burglarized, and I was forced to move again. As soon as I settled into my new place, I injured my knee and was unable to walk without pain. It was nearly nine months before I could *lightly* jog again. Then I sprained a hamstring! I also battled digestive issues and broke a tooth somewhere along the way. I dealt with feelings of inadequacy and unworthiness, stared fear and insecurity in the face, and warred against doubt and unbelief. The transparent truth is that this assignment was much bigger than me. It was absolutely impossible without the help of a loving, purposeful Creator. That is when you know it is His will. I constantly had to surrender my own timing, ability, and desires to His perfect leadership and plan. It is only in that place of letting go that the Holy Spirit can take over and use you the way He truly designed you to be used.

Writing this book was my full-time job for an entire year. I had to completely depend on God for provision every step of the way. I struggled to stay focused on my writing while also being available for family and friends who were dealing with injuries and illnesses. Many times I thought I was in the home stretch, and then I would find myself facing another setback. As soon as the final editor completed the edits on the manuscript, for example, and I was rejoicing in my soon-to-be-victory, I started having crazy heart palpitations that put me in the hospital overnight. I was frightened and uncomfortable, and for the first time in my life, I told the Lord that I was ready to come home if He was ready to take me. Once again, all I could do was *wait* and *trust*. I recalled what a friend told me a few years ago, when I was in a similarly stressful season: "This *setback* is just a *setup* for your *comeback.*" So I pressed on.

When I began to write, I *expected* to be tested, but I was not fully *prepared* for the circumstances I faced along the way. I was living completely by faith—wholly and humbly surrendered to the Lord. Each of these challenges caused me to draw closer to God in a unique way. The Teacher has been silent at times throughout this process. I had to take a few tests over to learn the lessons I needed to learn. I occasionally threatened to "drop out" and give up. But by God's grace and with His help, I ran the race and finished strong. Now I have a testimony that will prayerfully inspire others to stay the course, even in the midst of tremendous adversity. God is faithful. In all things and at all times, He is *good.*

I have learned that this life is about the journey more so than the finish line. I believe God is more concerned about the *process* than the *pace.* Being able to tell someone that you have "been there and done that" when they are struggling or to "keep the faith" when they are on the brink of letting go is worth the fight.

This race will not always be *easy* to run, but I can assure you that it will always be *worth* it. The Apostle Paul reminds us to ". . . run with endurance the race that is set before us, looking unto Jesus, the author and finisher of our faith . . . ." With each new obstacle I encountered as I wrote this book, my faith increased by leaps and bounds. I can say that the blood of Jesus set me free every second of every day as I committed my plans and time to Him. The deeper I go in my understanding of who He is, the more freedom I experience. Jesus longs to reveal His heart through the most minute of details on a continual basis. As long as we keep our eyes on Him, we *cannot* fail.

Your testimony, like Paul's, is a record of the way the blood of Jesus establishes your identity and empowers you to overcome the enemy in every area of your life. Revelation 12:11 says, "And they overcame him by the blood of the Lamb and by the word of their testimony, and they did not love their lives to the death." Once you taste His goodness, it will be a secret that you cannot keep. Tell the world how Jesus saved you and changed your life! Each time you do, it will remind you of His love for you, awakening your heart to fresh encounters with the living God. Isn't it wonderful how God turns your misery into your ministry, your mess into your message, and your test into your testimony? Share your story with someone today. You will be refreshed and revived as you remember His faithfulness and love in your life.

Pause and Reflect

Have you ever shared your testimony? Spend some time thinking about the entirety of your journey with God and how the blood of Jesus is incorporated throughout your story.

_____

_____

_____

_____

_____

_____

_____

_____

_____

_____

Raw and Real

God does not give you a testimony so you can keep it to yourself.

Short and Sweet

Jesus, I pray that every test will lead me closer to You. Reveal Yourself to me in ways that I have not known. Help me draw near to Your heart in every trial and use it all for Your glory. Amen.

Meditate and Memorize

"Now it happened, when I returned to Jerusalem and was praying in the temple, that I was in a trance and saw Him saying to me, 'Make haste and get out of Jerusalem quickly, for they will not receive your testimony concerning Me.'"
—Acts 22:17-18

Believe and Receive

I will share my testimony with others.

Listen and Learn
Condense your testimony here.

Create and Relate
Use this space to connect with God through creativity.

ACTS 23
DAY TWENTY-THREE

CHEER

θαρσέω

tharseō

thar-seh'-o

to have courage;
be of good comfort

The enemy of your soul is relentless. His primary objective is to steal, kill, and destroy everything that God has placed within you. When you pursue the heart of God with an undying passion and determination to fulfill your destiny, you become a terrible threat to the kingdom of darkness. This is not something to be afraid of, rather something to delight in and embrace. It is a wonderful privilege to be used by God!

One of the greatest weapons Satan is wielding against the people of God in this hour of history is depression. He is stealing the confidence, courage, and joy that have been promised to all who follow Christ. A depressed, lethargic Christian is incapable of revealing the strength and power of Almighty God in any circumstance. Someone who rarely smiles and does not abide in the joy of the Lord is not able to be the best witness he or she can be. Allow me to clarify here that hard times come upon us all. Everyone is subjected to emotional difficulty throughout the course of a lifetime. The problem is not our emotions, rather which ones we choose to meditate on and which ones we allow to consume us.

The Apostle Paul serves as an excellent example of this. He was beaten, imprisoned, tortured, mocked, ridiculed, and persecuted in every way. He was stoned, shipwrecked and faced death on numerous occasions, yet he never gave up. How is this possible?

Paul did not allow the fiery darts of the enemy to sabotage his joy. Perhaps he struggled. He was human. I imagine that he had moments of wrestling with God in his mind, will, and emotions as we all do. However, the way he responded to those times is what determined his victory. Paul discovered pure joy and abundant life in the revelation of who God is and what Jesus did for him. He recognized that he had been given the ability to stand strong in the face of all opposition through the power of the Holy Spirit. In John 10:10, Jesus reminds

> "I have come that they may have life, and that they may have it more abundantly."
>
> John 10:10

us, "The thief does not come except to steal, and to kill, and to destroy. I have come that they may have life, and that they may have it more abundantly." Abundant life is found in the outstretched arms of a Savior who died for your freedom. When you experience true liberty in Christ, there is an abiding joy that accompanies His holy presence.

A former pastor of mine often said, "You can't stop the birds from flying over your head, but you can stop them from building nests in your hair." Satan will always attempt to set up camp in your mind with negative thoughts, ungodly emotions, and distress of any kind. The word of God is your greatest weapon in this war being waged against your life and health.

In Acts 23:11, as Paul's life was being threatened yet again, Jesus appeared to him and urged him to "Be of good cheer." The word *cheer* in that verse is a Greek word that means to have courage, take comfort, and be confidently cheerful. The Lord was essentially telling Paul, "I am in control. Relax. I've got this. Trust Me." Oh, how we all wish it were that easy, right? This is why it is important to note that the word "cheer" is not a flippant attempt to calm Paul's nerves. Jesus was not patting Paul on the back with a casual "It's going to be okay" in the moments before he would presumably be ambushed and killed. Instead, it was a comforting exhortation by the Warrior King to be valiant and lionhearted, resting completely in the strength of his Defender.

The Bible tells us in Nehemiah 8:10, "Do not sorrow, for the joy of the Lord is your strength." I encourage you to meditate on that Scripture in times of sadness or despair. Sing it out loud and fix your heart on the goodness of God. It is impossible to prayerfully contemplate the joy of the Lord and not obtain His strength in the process. This is the power of the word of God. Do you remember when Paul and Silas were praying and singing hymns to the Lord at midnight while they were in prison?[66] They praised God even in their affliction. They allowed the joy of the Lord to alleviate the potential for depression and fear to consume them in those moments.

---

[66] Acts 16:25

James 1:2-3 says, "My brethren, count it all joy when you fall into various trials, knowing that the testing of your faith produces patience." The Greek word for *patience* in that verse is *hypomonē*, and it means "cheerful or hopeful endurance." Think about that. The testing of your faith produces cheerful or hopeful endurance. There is a testing of faith that occurs in any trial. This is part of the process of maturity as a Christian. It is a required aspect of growing in intimacy with a loving Father who wants to be known and trusted by His children. Your faith in God will actually increase when you learn to let cheerfulness and calm delight take the place of worry and doubt in the midst of difficulty. God is faithful and trustworthy. He wants you to have courage and good cheer as you let go and let Him be God.

The Lord knew that there would be an opportunity for Paul to be afraid of the impending threats against his life in Acts 23. He graciously revealed Himself to remind Paul that he was not alone. I marvel at the thought of Jesus standing by Paul's side and speaking to him in those moments. He could have told him anything. He did not give him an elaborate speech to deliver, nor did He supernaturally release him from the hands of his oppressors as He had done before. Instead, He chose to speak one simple little phrase to Paul that was guaranteed to give him peace as he stared death in the face. I believe He wanted Paul to know Him in this way at a deeper level. Rather than giving him an easy way out, Jesus extended an opportunity for Paul to grow in intimacy and trust.

> *"Do not sorrow, for the joy of the Lord is your strength."*
>
> *Nehemiah 8:10*

Have you ever been in a challenging situation and wondered if you would be able to make it through? Imagine that your best friend walks up to you when you are at your weakest point and says, "You can do it! You've still got a lot left in you. You are more than a conqueror!" Sometimes that is exactly the boost you need to carry you to the other side of a trial that seems like it could be the end of you.

Psalm 16:11 says, "You will show me the path of life; in Your presence is fullness of joy; at Your right hand are pleasures forevermore." If the joy of the Lord is your strength, and joy can be found in His presence, then we can rightly deduct that there is strength in His presence as well. That is where you must remain. His presence is your refuge and safe haven in the midst of the raging war that is going on all around you. Your circumstances should not dictate your attitude. Take every thought captive. Do not allow those wicked birds of prey to roost in your mind. Replace a defeatist mindset with affirmations from the word of God. Praise Him in the storm!

As God commissioned Joshua to lead the Israelites into the Promised Land, one of the first things He told him was to "Be strong and of good courage . . . ."[67] In fact, He knew that it was not going to be easy, so He told him twice in two verses! That is exactly the same message that Paul needed to hear in Acts 23, and it is what we all need to hear during various seasons of difficulty. Be strong and very courageous. You can do all things *through* Christ who strengthens you![68] Be of good cheer, beloved! God is with you.

---

[67] Joshua 1:6-7
[68] Philippians 4:13

Pause and Reflect

As you go forward, how will the words of Christ to Paul in this chapter affect the way you will approach trials in your own life?

_____

_____

_____

_____

_____

_____

_____

_____

_____

_____

_____

Raw and Real

Grumbling and complaining seem to be the default responses to struggles among Christians today.

Short and Sweet

Joyful Lord, thank You that Your joy is an abiding fountain that strengthens me at all times. Remind me to live in that place. Holy Spirit, increase the fruit of joy in my life so that all may see You in me. Amen.

Meditate and Memorize

"But the following night the Lord stood by him and said, 'Be of good cheer, Paul; for as you have testified for Me in Jerusalem, so you must also bear witness at Rome.'"
—Acts 23:11

Believe and Receive

The joy of the Lord is my strength.

Listen and Learn
Seek His presence and receive His joy.

Create and Relate
Use this space to connect with God through creativity.

ACTS 24
DAY TWENTY-FOUR

HOPE

ἐλπις

elpis

el-pece'

faith;
expectation or confidence;
to anticipate, usually with pleasure

We are living in an age where hope is a hot topic. You will find it in campaign slogans and hear about it in religious crusades. People all around the world are grasping at anything and everything to give them hope. I have news for you. Lasting hope can only be found in Jesus Christ, and in the eternal promises of His word. There is no hope outside of knowing Him.

If I were to ask you to explain hope, could you do it? Many people can readily describe a sense of hopelessness. They can easily express the despair that dwells within a hopeless heart. When asked to discuss hope, however, there seems to be an inability to reach within and articulate it—especially if one does not possess a living hope in Christ. What exactly is hope? Where does it come from and how can we obtain it?

A world-renowned religious leader once said, "The one who has hope lives differently." People are desperate for change. There is a spiritual battle raging over the life of every individual on earth. Even the mightiest of warriors are wounded, weary, and losing hope. The Lord sent me to remind you that *HE* is your hope. When everything seems to be falling apart, you still have hope in Christ. Hopelessness can only occur when you do not know (or you forget) who you are, why you are here, or where you are going when you leave this life. Once you believe and receive the truth about your identity according to God's word, you will begin to experience the reality of hope. Your circumstances will no longer dictate your attitude when hope abides in your heart.

> *When everything seems to be falling apart, you still have hope in Christ.*

Acts 24 gives us insight into a heart that is filled with hope. Paul was being accused before Felix, the Roman governor of Judea. Tertullus claimed that the Apostle had caused great trouble worldwide as a captain of the Christians. He berated Paul with blatant lies. He charged that Paul was guilty of sacrilege, stating that he had desecrated the temple; yet Paul was not deterred. Paul defended himself by explaining that the Jews were hostile toward him because of a difference in religious beliefs and not because of any wrongdoing on his part. He proceeded to describe his worship of the one true God, the God of Abraham, Isaac, and Jacob. Then He revealed the hope he had in God alone because of the *doctrine of the resurrection of the dead.*

What is this doctrine and how does it inspire hope in us as Christians? First of all, a doctrine is simply a belief, teaching, or precept. According to Paul, the only hope for the dead is a resurrection hope. He puts it this way in Acts 24:15, "I have hope in God, which they themselves also accept, that there will be a resurrection of the dead, both of the just and the unjust." Jesus Christ *is* the hope of resurrection. This is something that Paul acknowledged and boldly declared before the leaders in Caesarea. In his letter to the Philippians, Paul stated, "For to me, to live is Christ, and to die is gain."[69] In other words, my hope is *in Him* either way.

Hope is not simply wishful thinking. It is confident expectation. It is a desire and anticipation for a certain thing to happen. Hope is associated with dreams, goals, plans, and aspirations. It involves optimism, assurance, promise, and possibility. Without hope, life is less than full. With hope, life is overflowing.

As Christians, our hope is found *in Christ.* We have hope that all of God's promises are fulfilled in Jesus. We have hope in eternal life and a royal inheritance as heirs of God and joint heirs with Christ.[70] According to Titus 2:11-14, "For the grace of God that brings salvation has appeared to all men, teaching us that, denying ungodliness and worldly lusts, we should live soberly, righteously, and godly in the present age, looking for the blessed hope and glorious appearing of our great God and Savior Jesus Christ, who gave Himself for us, that He might redeem us from every lawless deed and purify for Himself His own special people, zealous for good works."

---

[69]   Philippians 1:21
[70]   Romans 8:16-17

Like faith, hope is placed in something that cannot be seen with natural eyes. Romans 8:24-25 says, "For we were saved in this hope, but hope that is seen is not hope; for why does one still hope for what he sees? But if we hope for what we do not see, we eagerly wait for it with perseverance." The presence of God, the kingdom of God, and the reality of God are all unseen aspects of a relationship with God. We must train ourselves to see with our spiritual eyes what God has promised to His children. Hope abounds as we begin to see things as God sees them.

Ephesians 3:20 reminds us that God is *able*! It says, "Now to Him who is able to do exceedingly abundantly above all that we ask or think, according to the power that works in us, to Him be glory in the church by Christ Jesus to all generations, forever and ever. Amen." Unfortunately, many of God's chosen ones are bound by hopelessness. They do not truly believe that He is an Ephesians 3:20 God. They have forgotten the power of His presence and the promises of His word. They are weak and distraught from waiting. They have dreams that never came to fruition. They have given up on the possibility of the promises God made. They doubt that He is faithful, and they choose the path of least resistance rather than maintain hope.

Does your hope need to be resurrected today? For what are you eagerly waiting, as Romans 8:25 says? Are you waiting with perseverance? Or do you hopelessly exist apart from the promises of God in your life? I remember a specific word God gave me several years ago regarding the greatest desire of my heart. At first, I stood on His promise with a seemingly unshakable determination. I prayed, I contended, I believed, and I waited. One year turned into two, two turned into three, and three turned into seven! At this writing, I am still waiting!

> *Hope abounds as we begin to see things as God sees them.*

Over the course of seven years, I have wavered, faltered, and nearly given up. In fact, many times I basically told God to "Forget it!" I found myself wanting to settle for less to ease the pain of hopelessness that overwhelmed my heart and life in this particular area. At times, I compromised. I doubted God. But He continues to graciously draw me back to His word and remind me that He is *able*. He whispers Jeremiah 29:11 to me, "For I know the thoughts that I think toward you, says the Lord, thoughts of peace and not of evil, to give you a future and a hope." And He simply says, "Trust Me."

Trusting God in the waiting is sometimes easier said than done. Hopelessness speaks contrary to the promises of God in our lives. It says, "It will never happen" or "God is not that good" or "He does not love you that much." Hopelessness will even deceive you into thinking that you do not know God's voice at all. However, when God is in it, something inside of you will rise up and fight for what He has promised. Nothing else will satisfy you outside of the great and marvelous promises of the Lord. So you eagerly wait, with perseverance, placing your hope in what is currently unseen and believing that you will eventually see it come to pass. Numbers 23:19 says, "God is not a man, that He should lie, nor a son of man, that He should repent. Has He said, and will He not do? Or has He spoken, and will He not make it good?" In other words, if God said it, that settles it.

I know many people who have buried their dreams. They have given up on fulfilling or pursuing the promises God gave them. As a result, they have settled for less than God's best in their lives. They have become content with complacency and mediocrity, and they no longer want to "get their hopes up." We have all been there at some point, fighting feelings of frustration and disappointment. We have submitted to the lies of the adversary that are intended to steal, kill, and destroy all that God has promised. Like Abraham and Sarah, we have laughed in disbelief and mocked the word of God.[71] We have even waved our proverbial white flags in surrender. Unfortunately, we have surrendered our hope and faith in what God has promised, rather than surrendering our will and timing to His.

I have good news! You serve the God of "GET YOUR HOPES UP!" He placed desires inside of you as He formed you in your mother's womb.[72] Imagine the impossible! Your heavenly

---

[71] Genesis 17:17, 18:12

[72] Psalm 139

Father takes pleasure in making the impossible possible. You are not forgotten, beloved. You are cherished and adored. You have been promised a future and a hope beyond your wildest imagination. 1 Corinthians 2:9 says, "Eye has not seen, nor ear heard, nor have entered into the heart of man the things which God has prepared for those who love Him." Dream BIG!

I was one of those people who did not want to ask too much or hope for too much from God. I feared that He may say "No," and I would be disappointed. I had to allow Him to renew my mind in this area so I could dream again. I had to believe that He is a good Father who delights in blessing His children. Psalm 37:4-5 encourages me. It says, "Delight yourself also in the Lord, and He shall give you the desires of your heart. Commit your way to the Lord, trust also in Him, and He shall bring it to pass." He *shall* give you the desires of your heart. He *shall* bring it to pass. Not *maybe* or *possibly*, but *definitely*. The conditions for that promise are simple—delight yourself in the Lord, commit your way to Him, and trust in Him. He will do the rest.

Some of your aspirations and dreams may be fleshly pursuits, but there are others that God placed within you. When you delight yourself in the Lord, His desires become your desires, and your desires become His desires. As you spend time with Him in the secret place, laying all of your goals and plans before Him, you will begin to discern His will. *Do not be afraid to dream.* Just do it from the place of intimacy, identity, and purpose in Him. Be mindful of selfish ambitions and impure motives. Choose to consecrate your life in purity and holiness to the One who is able to make all of your dreams come true. Hope abounds in His faithfulness.

> *"Delight yourself also in the Lord, and He shall give you the desires of your heart."*
>
> *Psalm 37:4*

1 Peter 3:15 instructs believers to ". . . always be ready to give a defense to everyone who asks you a reason for the hope that is in you . . . ." This is what Paul did as he stood before his accusers in Acts 24. He boldly declared that he had placed

his hope in God and in the promise of resurrection. He lived differently. He did not allow fear or confusion to overwhelm him at a time when most people would cower under the pressure. He was absolutely certain that what he knew about Jesus was true. He faithfully proclaimed to unbelieving Jews that he had hope, and he proved it by the way he lived his life.

Proverbs 23:18 says, "For surely there is a hereafter, and your hope will not be cut off." Hope heals the aching soul. Sometimes hope is all you have left. When life appears to be crumbling around you, your hope in Christ will provide a steadfast anchor for your soul. [73] It is that very hope that keeps a believer securely fastened to the love and purposes of God.

Hope heals the aching soul.

Even in the midst of tragedy and crisis, Paul believed the promises of God. He had hope in what was unseen. He trusted that God had a great future prepared for him. Do you have that kind of hope? If so, you will transform your realm of influence daily. Hope keeps your fire burning as you wait for the return of Christ, and it makes other people want what you have. So get your hopes up! And let your light shine today and every day for His glory.

---

[73] Hebrews 6:19

Pause and Reflect

How would you respond if you were being wrongfully accused as Paul was? Consider how you will live differently because of the hope you have in Christ.

_____

_____

_____

_____

_____

_____

_____

_____

_____

_____

Raw and Real

Placing hope in the promises of man will never satisfy the longing for eternity that resides in the human heart.

Short and Sweet

Resurrected Lord, thank You for revealing the way to eternal life and giving me hope for a future spent with You. Help me remember that there is no hope apart from You. Remind me daily that You alone fulfill my greatest desires. Amen.

Meditate and Memorize

"I have hope in God, which they themselves also accept, that there will be a resurrection of the dead, both of the just and the unjust."
—Acts 24:15

Believe and Receive

My hope is in Christ.

Listen and Learn

Share your hopes and desires with God.

_____

_____

_____

_____

_____

_____

_____

_____

_____

_____

_____

_____

_____

_____

_____

_____

_____

_____

_____

_____

_____

_____

_____

_____

_____

_____

_____

_____

_____

_____

_____

_____

_____

_____

Create and Relate

Use this space to connect with God through creativity.

JESUS

Ἰησοῦς

Iēsous

ee-ay-sooce'

the Son of God;
God in human form;
the Savior of mankind;
the name of our Lord;
of Hebrew origin:
"Jehovah is salvation"

Jesus is the most beautiful and controversial name in history. It is the name that sets captives free and causes the most wicked of men to fall to their knees. It is the name of the One who made a way for all to enter the presence of a loving God. In Acts 25, the name of Jesus is mentioned only one time, but it is enough to remind us that He is the very reason Paul is standing accused before the leaders of the land.

Reading through the book of Acts is indeed an adventure-filled experience. It is an interesting journey through the lives of those who became the first followers of Christ. Miracles, signs, and wonders abound. Exceeding joy and forgiveness are expressed in the midst of torture, death, and imprisonment. Men and women of God work, travel, teach, preach, and break bread together. There is a lot going on in this book that is so appropriately dubbed "Acts." However, it is important to remember that none of this would be happening apart from the Lord Jesus Christ and the power that resides in His name.

What is it about that name that is so offensive to unbelievers? The phrase "Lord Jesus Christ" is used over one hundred times in the New Testament. A better understanding of this complete name of God will expose the reasons why His disciples face so much opposition from those who do not know Him.

The title, *"Lord,"* refers to the *personal relationship* God has with those He has saved. His human name, *"Jesus,"* serves as a constant reminder that He left His abode in heaven to come to earth as a *mortal man.* The word *"Christ"* comes from the Greek word *Christos* and is the equivalent of the Hebrew word for Messiah. It means *"Anointed One,"* and it identifies Him as *Prophet, Priest, and King.*

> *Jesus is the most beautiful and controversial name in history.*

Can you see why the Jews were outraged because of Paul's belief in the Lord Jesus Christ? The religious hypocrites who were accusing him did not know Jesus as *"Lord"* because they rejected Him as Savior. They were offended by the name *"Jesus"* because it implied that God became a man, which they considered to be blasphemous. Finally, they disputed the title of *"Christ"* because they were still waiting for their coming Messiah.

Jesus said in Luke 9:26, "For whoever is ashamed of Me and My words, of him the Son of Man will be ashamed when He comes in His own glory, and in His Father's, and of the holy angels." Throughout the book of Acts, the disciples were bold witnesses for the King of kings and the Lord of lords, Jesus Christ. They were not fearful of mentioning His name, nor were they ashamed to declare their loyalty to Him. Paul found himself in the midst of people who threatened his life on a consistent basis; yet he boldly proclaimed the truth about Jesus. He did not use vague terminology to describe the One he loved, nor did he abstain from discussions pertaining to salvation. He believed in the power and authority of the name of Jesus, and he preached with a confident assurance of that reality. For this reason, God allowed him to stand in the presence of high profile leaders, sharing his testimony and continually being a witness for Christ.

Philippians 2:9-11 says, "Therefore God also has highly exalted Him and given Him the name which is above every name, that at the name of Jesus every knee should bow, of those in heaven, and of those on earth, and of those under the earth, and that every tongue should confess that Jesus Christ is Lord, to the glory of God the Father." God specifically selected the name *Jesus* for a reason. It means "Jehovah is salvation." Names are very significant in the Bible and in our own lives. A name identifies you and speaks destiny over you. If you do not know what your name means, I encourage you to find out. What are people saying about you when they call your name?

God is in the business of giving new names to His children who have been inappropriately identified. For example, in Genesis 32:28-29, God told Jacob, "Your name shall no longer be called Jacob, but Israel; for you have struggled with God and with men, and have prevailed." Whereas *Jacob* means *supplanter* (one who wrongfully or illegally seizes and holds the place of another), God chose to call Him *Israel*, which literally translates as *Prince with God.* It also means *God prevails.* Likewise, Paul's name was originally Saul, but it was changed to Paul in order to better connect him to his destiny. His former name, *Saul,* was associated with negative images of evil and brutality. His new name, *Paul,* means *"small,"* and it gives a clear perspective of the humility he felt before his awesome God as a new creation in Christ.

Jesus is not simply another name. It is *the name above every other name,* and it was chosen by God to identify Him as Savior. Unfortunately, His name has been abused in modern culture. We need to use it respectfully and with great honor.

Hebrews 12:1-2 encourages believers, "Therefore we also, since we are surrounded by so great a cloud of witnesses, let us lay aside every weight, and the sin which so easily ensnares us, and let us run with endurance the race that is set before us, looking unto Jesus, the author and finisher of our faith, who for the joy that was set before Him endured the cross, despising the shame, and has sat down at the right hand of the throne of God." The Apostle Paul had his eyes fixed on Jesus at all times and in every circumstance. He not only trusted in the name, but He also believed in the Son of God—the *Man* Jesus—who died for him. *Jesus* was the reason Paul faced so much adversity. It was God in the flesh that Paul fearlessly worshiped and adored. This is why he could confidently say in 1 Corinthians 11:1, "Imitate me, just as I also imitate Christ."

Who is Jesus to you? Would you profess him before a council of elders? Would you joyfully take your last breath as you were being crucified because of His name? Would you stand before an unbelieving king and declare the truth? Would you defend Christ, even if it cost you friendships and popularity?

Who is Jesus to you?

This book would be incomplete without a chapter that magnifies the name of Jesus. Take some time to meditate on the Lord Jesus Christ. Think about His word, His life, His death, His burial, His resurrection, His ascension, and His return. Consider His sacrifice for you and for all mankind. Imagine what He went through in the final moments of His life as He gave Himself up for your sins.

Jesus loves you. He is the answer to every question you will ever have. He is the solution to every problem you will ever face. He carries you and holds your hand in your greatest times of need. He never leaves your side. He is strength, hope, grace, and joy. He is forgiveness, purity, light, and love. He is incomprehensible beauty, an all-consuming fire, and the rushing river of life. He is Savior, Redeemer, Bridegroom, and Friend. He is Mighty Warrior and Prince of Peace. He is eternal glory and everlasting truth. He is Spirit, power, freedom, and assurance. He is your greatest advocate and your biggest fan. He is your mighty refuge, ultimate defender, comforting counselor, and faithful provider. He is the sinless, spotless Lamb who was slain so you could draw near to God. He is everything you will ever need, and to know Him is to never be the same. Every knee shall bow before Him. Let it be yours today.

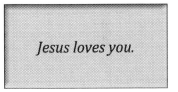

Jesus loves you.

Pause and Reflect

Meditate on the Lord Jesus Christ. Have you ever been ashamed of His name? How will you reverence His name going forward?

_____

_____

_____

_____

_____

_____

_____

_____

_____

_____

Raw and Real

Jesus Christ is not a curse word.

Short and Sweet

Thank You, loving Father, for the name that causes knees to bow and hearts to change. Please forgive me for any time I have been ashamed of You or used Your name in vain. I pray for the boldness to faithfully declare Your name before all men all the days of my life. Amen.

Meditate and Memorize

"When the accusers stood up, they brought no accusation against him of such things as I supposed, but had some questions against him about their own religion and about a certain Jesus, who had died, whom Paul affirmed to be alive."
—Acts 25:18-19

Believe and Receive

Jesus is the name above every name.

Listen and Learn

Ask Jesus to reveal Himself to you.

Create and Relate
Use this space to connect with God through creativity.

ACTS 26
DAY TWENTY-SIX

INHERITANCE

κλῆρος

klēros

klay'-ros

lot, part, heritage;
an acquisition, especially from
one's father or male ancestor

You are an heir to the throne of God. You have an inheritance in His kingdom, and through the blood of Jesus you have been perfectly positioned to acquire the portion allotted to you. A Christian's inheritance is a share of the eternal blessings of the kingdom of God. As God's children, we are also His heirs. According to Romans 8:16-17, "The Spirit Himself bears witness with our spirit that we are children of God, and if children, then heirs—heirs of God and joint heirs with Christ, if indeed we suffer with Him, that we may also be glorified together."

In Paul's exposition before King Agrippa in Acts 26:6-7, he stated, "And now I stand and am judged for the hope of the promise made by God to our fathers. To this promise our twelve tribes, earnestly serving God night and day, hope to attain. For this hope's sake, King Agrippa, I am accused by the Jews." Paul was being persecuted because he had hope in the promise of an eternal inheritance with Christ. As he recounted his conversion on the road to Damascus in Acts 26:18, he shared the promise Jesus made of ". . . an inheritance among those who are sanctified by faith in Me." What exactly is this inheritance and how does it affect your identity as a living heir today?

Ephesians 1:3-6 says, "Blessed be the God and Father of our Lord Jesus Christ, who has blessed us with every spiritual blessing in the heavenly places in Christ, just as He chose us in Him before the foundation of the world, that we should be holy and without blame before Him in love, having predestined us to adoption as sons by Jesus Christ to Himself, according to the good pleasure of His will, to the praise of the glory of His grace, by which He made us accepted in the Beloved." The Father of our Lord Jesus Christ has adopted you as His son or daughter, and it is His good pleasure to give you an inheritance in Christ.

> *You are an heir to the throne of God.*

Romans 8:14-15 says, "For as many as are led by the Spirit of God, these are sons of God. For you did not receive the spirit of bondage again to fear, but you received the Spirit of adoption by whom we cry out, 'Abba, Father.'" The Holy

Spirit, the Spirit of adoption, moves you to call on God as Abba, Father. As His child, you receive eternal love and acceptance. You will never feel orphaned again once you understand that you have been adopted into the family of God.

From a practical perspective, adopted children may be grafted into a family's will or "testament" as though they were biologically related to the person with the estate. Through the blood of Jesus, at salvation, you supernaturally become "biologically related" to God. This makes you privy to all that belongs to Him. You are no longer "disinherited" because of sin. Instead, the blood of Jesus qualifies you for what you would not otherwise obtain. Hebrews 9:16-17 informs us, "For where there is a testament, there must also of necessity be the death of the testator. For a testament is in force after men are dead, since it has no power at all while the testator lives." A testament is a contract or covenant identifying the disposition of someone's possessions after death. The New Testament, therefore, came into being after the death of Jesus. The shed blood of Christ formed a new covenant, allowing all of God's children to partake in His kingdom possessions—both now and forever.

According to James 1:17, "Every good gift and every perfect gift is from above, and comes down from the Father of lights, with whom there is no variation or shadow of turning." We serve a God who delights in blessing His children here on earth. How much more will He bless them in eternity! God is the possessor of heaven and earth and everything in them. As the Creator and Owner of all things seen and unseen, He will share with His children what is rightfully His. So what exactly is your inheritance as a blood-bought child of the King of glory?

The following italicized phrases reveal your Scriptural inheritance as a member of God's family: you have been blessed *"with every spiritual blessing in the heavenly places"* (Ephesians 1:3); *"you will receive the reward of the inheritance; for you serve the Lord Christ"* (Colossians 3:24); you are a joint heir with Christ of *"all things"* (Hebrews 1:2, Revelation 21:7); you *"shall inherit the earth"* (Matthew 5:5); you *"shall receive a hundredfold, and inherit eternal life"* (Matthew 19:29); you will be an heir *"of the kingdom which He promised to those who love Him"* (James 2:5).

Many of these Scripture references include conditional or qualifying statements from the Lord. For example, Matthew 5:5 states, "Blessed are the meek, for they shall inherit the earth." I encourage you to study the above verses on your own, paying attention to the specific actions, attributes, and heart postures that are mentioned.

The following passages regarding inheritance are from the book of Revelation and are addressed to the one *"who overcomes:"* *"eat from the tree of life, which is in the midst of the Paradise of God"* (Revelation 2:7); given *"power over the nations"* (Revelation 2:26); *"shall be clothed in white garments, and I will not blot out his name from the Book of Life; but I will confess his name before My Father and before His angels"* (Revelation 3:5); *"I will grant to sit with Me on My throne, as I also overcame and sat down with My Father on His throne"* (Revelation 3:21). Finally, Revelation 5:9-10 reminds us that we have been redeemed to God by the blood of Jesus and have been made kings and priests who shall reign on the earth.

Hebrews 1:4 says that Jesus "has by inheritance obtained a more excellent name" than the angels. As part of your inheritance and as a reward for being victorious in Christ, God will also make your name great—not necessarily through worldly fame, but by writing it in the Lamb's Book of Life.[74]

The seal of the Holy Spirit on your life is a guarantee of your inheritance in the kingdom of God and a promise that your name will be listed as an heir forever. Ephesians 1:13-14 assures us, "In Him you also trusted, after you heard the word of truth, the gospel of your salvation; in whom also, having believed, you were sealed with the Holy Spirit of promise, who is the guarantee of our inheritance until the redemption of the purchased possession, to the praise of His glory." The Holy Spirit is your down payment on earth for what God has promised in eternity. In heaven, you will receive the full reward of His presence and glory. You will see Him face to face and spend everlasting life dwelling with Him because you have been

---

[74] Revelation 3:5

marked with the seal of His Spirit. Though man does not physically see this seal of divine ownership, it is recognized by all in the light of eternity and identifies you as a child of God.

Remember that you are God's purchased possession. The blood of Jesus has redeemed you and made you an heir through adoption. He no longer calls you a slave, but a son or a daughter. As His offspring, you have access to all that is His. In John 14:2, Jesus said, "In My Father's house are many mansions; if it were not so, I would have told you. I go to prepare a place for you." That heavenly place is your inheritance. It is a special place in the abode of God where there is no more sin, no more heartache, no more hunger, no more hatred, and no more warfare. It is a peaceful place prepared by a loving Father for His beloved children.

> *The Holy Spirit is your down payment on earth for what God has promised in eternity.*

Hebrews 11:6 tells us that God ". . . is a rewarder of those who diligently seek Him." He rewards His children by inviting them to spend eternity in His presence partaking of everything good and glorious. Paul understood that his inheritance stretched far beyond his natural sight and comprehension. He lived a life of power and authority because he *knew who he was*, and he *believed the promises of God*. This is barely scratching the surface of what is in store for those who are called heirs of the Most High God. Paul's life-changing revelation of his identity and inheritance in Christ propelled him forward in the most trying circumstances. As he presented his testimony in Acts 26, the Bible tells us that the king was "almost persuaded" to become a Christian.[75] Whether the king received the promises of God in eternity is yet to be known, but we can all rest assured that Paul will enjoy his portion. Will you?

---

[75] Acts 26:28

Pause and Reflect

How does the knowledge of your inheritance as a child of God affect the way you view yourself?

_____

_____

_____

_____

_____

_____

_____

_____

_____

_____

Raw and Real

Earthly possessions pale in comparison to what God has promised His children in His word.

Short and Sweet

Loving Father, thank You for making a way for me to spend eternity with You. Continue to speak to me about the inheritance I have been promised in Christ and teach me how to live accordingly. Amen.

Meditate and Memorize

". . . to open their eyes, in order to turn them from darkness to light, and from the power of Satan to God, that they may receive forgiveness of sins and an inheritance among those who are sanctified by faith in Me."
—Acts 26:18

Believe and Receive

Everything that is His is mine.

Listen and Learn
Meditate on your identity as an heir of God.

_____

_____

_____

_____

_____

_____

_____

_____

_____

_____

_____

_____

_____

_____

_____

_____

_____

_____

_____

_____

_____

_____

_____

_____

_____

_____

_____

_____

_____

_____

_____

_____

_____

_____

_____

_____

_____

_____

_____

_____

_____

Create and Relate
Use this space to connect with God through creativity.

ACTS 27
DAY TWENTY-SEVEN

BELIEVE

πιστεύω

pisteuō

pist-yoo'-o

to think to be true;
to be persuaded of;
to entrust or commit to trust;
to credit or place confidence in;
to have faith in a person or thing

Jesus promised that nothing would be impossible for you if you would only believe.[76] Imagine that you were on that ship with Paul and 275 other people in Acts 27. How would you react to the storms and difficulties they encountered on their voyage? Would you be grumbling, complaining, and frightened or would you be on your knees in prayer, believing that God was in control?

Humanity lends itself to fear. It is the curse of the fallen nature and one of the weapons Satan uses to sabotage your life. Your adversary does not want you to operate in the liberty that accompanies absolute faith in Jesus Christ. The enemy of your soul does not want you to discover your true identity as a blood-bought, Spirit-filled believer who has access to all that is God's. When you *believe* you are who God says you are, you become a mighty warrior in His great army. You arise as a valiant soldier able to stand against all opposition. You are engaged in a battle between good and evil on a daily basis, surrounded by spiritual warfare in the unseen realms. The good news is that Jesus died for your victory. It is finished. All you have to do is believe.

God has already provided everything you need to accomplish all that He has called you to be and do in this life. He will not ask you to give what you do not have. He will only ask you to give what you have already been given. He is El Shaddai, the All-Sufficient One. He lives

> *Jesus promised that nothing would be impossible for you if you would only believe.*

within you through His Holy Spirit. He sustains, equips, and establishes you. Your identity is *in Him*. Jesus said, "With God all things are possible."[77] Do you believe Him?

You are a stranger and foreigner in this world. You have been chosen to fulfill a specific assignment issued to you by the Commander in Chief of heaven's armies. Consider yourself on a mission. There will be obstacles to overcome and battles to

[76] Matthew 17:20
[77] Matthew 19:26

fight along the way, but this mission is *possible*. You must not allow distractions or fear to prevent you from drawing near to Him in adversity. You can *choose* to accept and believe the promises of God intended to set you free instead of succumbing to the lies and deception of the evil one.

Paul was on a mission. He had a one-track mind. His heart and eyes were fixed on Jesus. He knew what he was called and created to do, and he did it with a fiery zeal that set the world ablaze. He weathered storms with tenacity and perseverance. He was a faithful servant of God, and he *believed* that he had nothing to fear. He knew that Jesus had already conquered death, hell, and the grave, destroying all fear and opening the door to everlasting life. Paul was determined to spend his time wisely and purposefully, loving God and loving people, even in the most challenging circumstances. He trusted in the One who chose him, and he did not veer to the left or to the right in pursuit of his destiny. Paul was a fireball. He said what the Lord told Him to say with no hesitation, and he endured tribulation with joyful anticipation of the Lord's intervention. A lifetime of lessons can be learned from this blessed man of God.

In Acts 27, Paul's life was once again being threatened. This time, it was the wind and the waves that jeopardized his mission. The Bible mentions the "difficulty" Paul faced on his voyage multiple times in this chapter. Look at the graphic terminology used to describe his circumstances in the following italicized phrases. Verse 4 says *the winds were contrary.* Verse 7 says they *arrived with difficulty* and goes on to say that *the wind did not permit them to proceed.* Verse 8 says they were passing the island of Crete *with difficulty.* Verse 9 says *sailing was dangerous.* Verse 14 says *a tempestuous head wind arose.* Verse 16 says they *secured the skiff with difficulty.* Verse 18 says they were *exceedingly tempest-tossed.* Twice, in verses 17 and 29, they *feared* that they would run aground. This does not sound like a fun little missionary excursion, does it? Paul and his shipmates confronted death in the center of a brutal storm that was clearly difficult for them to navigate.

Does that sound familiar? Have you ever found yourself dealing with an unwelcome and possibly unexpected turn of events that caused you to get off course or delayed your arrival at an intended destination? How did you respond? Did you moan and whine to God about how big your storm was or did you rebuke the wind and the waves, telling the storm how big your God is? Life is a voyage that carries you through various storms as you navigate your path to destiny. Seeking greater intimacy with God by living a purpose-filled life is not always easy. You must remember there is no victory without a battle; there is no rainbow without the rain; and there is no breakthrough without some obstacles and opposition.

Acts 27:14 says, "But not long after, a tempestuous head wind arose, called Euroclydon." *Euroclydon* is a Greek word that identifies a storm from the east. It literally means "a violent agitation." When you are sailing headlong into your purpose, discovering your identity in Christ, you will inevitably encounter violent agitations along the way. *Violent* agitations. These are not simply the daily irritations of life. These are the storms that are intended to shake your faith, fill you with fear, and ultimately destroy you. They are the mighty winds of change that could cause you to lose sight of your goals or convince you to give up. However, like Paul, these are the times to press in and *believe* God rather than run away from Him.

Unbelief, one violent agitation from the enemy, is assigned to your destiny from the moment you are born. It is a tempestuous head wind that arises just as you are about to cross over to the other side of a particular challenge or difficult situation. Paul exhorts us in 1 Timothy 6:12 to "fight the good fight of faith." In other words, *believe* God in the midst of the warfare. He is with you, even in the storms. He has a plan for your life, and He guarantees that it will come to pass if you trust and follow Him every step of the way. Everything the enemy meant for evil will be used for your good and for God's glory.[78]

In Matthew 11:12, Jesus said, "And from the days of John the Baptist until now the kingdom of heaven suffers violence, and the violent take it by force." The violent agitations you experience on your voyage will either make you or break you. The choice is yours. Will you merely *go* through it or will you

---

[78] Genesis 50:20

grow through it? Remember, you are equipped to withstand the storms that are in your path. It will be a rough ride at times. You may not be able to see two feet in front of you, but if you lean into God and take His hand, He will lead you safely to the other side.

Paul's life did not end in Acts 27. God had further plans for the Apostle in Rome, and not even the wicked Euroclydon could prevent him from arriving. Paul had to fast and pray a little harder to get there. He had to wait and trust a little more in the process. He had to struggle through a few detours along the way. Most importantly he had to *believe* God through it all.

There is a region of calm weather located in the center of every torrential tropical storm. This place of refuge, if you will, is known as "the eye of the storm." *Jesus* is the eye in the center of your raging storm. In the midst of life's cyclone of circumstances, you can find solace in His presence. He is your place of peace and rest. He will never abandon you. In your greatest times of need, Jesus is there. He says, "Peace, be still!" And the wind and waves obey.[79]

> *In your greatest times of need, Jesus is there.*

Paul had countless opportunities to doubt God in Acts 27. It would have been easy to wonder if he was out of God's will because of the resistance he faced. Yet God sent an angel to affirm that he was on the right path. Acts 27:23-25 says, "For there stood by me this night an angel of the God to whom I belong and whom I serve, saying, 'Do not be afraid, Paul; you must be brought before Caesar; and indeed God has granted you all those who sail with you.' Therefore take heart, men, for I believe God that it will be just as it was told me." One word from the Lord comforted Paul with the assurance of a safe arrival.

Do you believe that God is always faithful? Do you believe that His word is true? Do you stand on His promises and believe that He will accomplish them in your life? Jesus did not say that *some things* would be impossible for you on your

---

[79]   Mark 4:39

journey. He said *nothing* would be impossible *if you believe.* Think of how that must terrify the enemy. Oh, if you would only believe as Paul did! In every storm, in every trial, praise Him for His promises and thank Him for His faithfulness. Your ship may be wrecked from time to time, but that is only because God has a new, stronger vessel purposed to carry you on to your final destination. Do not be afraid, beloved. Only believe.

Pause and Reflect

What would your life look like if you really believed that God is who He says He is in His word? How would you make a difference in the lives of others if you possessed an abiding belief in the power and love of God?

_____

_____

_____

_____

_____

_____

_____

_____

_____

_____

_____

_____

Raw and Real

Unbelieving believers is an oxymoron.

Short and Sweet

Lord, heal my unbelief! You are the All-Sufficient One. Teach me how to rest in Your presence in the midst of every storm and battle. Help me trust You more. I want to walk by faith and not by sight, believing that nothing is impossible with You. Amen.

Meditate and Memorize

"Therefore take heart, men, for I believe God that it will be just as it was told me."
—Acts 27:25

Believe and Receive

I believe.

Listen and Learn

Confess any doubt, fear, or unbelief.

_____
_____
_____
_____
_____
_____
_____
_____
_____
_____
_____
_____
_____
_____
_____
_____
_____
_____
_____
_____
_____
_____
_____
_____
_____
_____
_____
_____
_____

Create and Relate
Use this space to connect with God through creativity.

ACTS 28
DAY TWENTY-EIGHT

FIRE

πυρὰ

pura

poo-rah'

a pile of burning fuel

You are a firestarter. You are the sanctuary and dwelling place of a holy God who has revealed Himself in fire throughout history. In the beginning God said, "Let there be light."[80] The word for *light* in that verse is derived from a Hebrew root word (רוֹא 'or) that literally means *to kindle or set on fire*. At the onset of creation, God kindled a fire. He sent a supernatural surge of power into a deep dark void and created something brilliant. His life-filled words caused a flood of heavenly luminaries to break forth like dawn and penetrate the unimaginable absence of light.

Genesis 1:2 says, "The earth was without form, and void; and darkness was on the face of the deep. And the Spirit of God was hovering over the face of the waters." You were no different than the earth in the beginning. You were without form and void. Darkness enveloped you before God spoke purpose, destiny, and identity into your very being. His Spirit hovered over you, and His majestic voice declared, "LET THERE BE LIGHT!" A fire was kindled. And there was light.

> *At the onset of creation, God kindled a fire.*

The Bible tells us that God is like a consuming fire. Exodus 24:17 says, "The sight of the glory of the Lord was like a consuming fire on the top of the mountain in the eyes of the children of Israel." In the Old Testament, God appeared to Moses ". . . in a flame of fire from the midst of a bush."[81] In the New Testament, the Holy Spirit appeared to the disciples in fire on the Day of Pentecost: "Then there appeared to them divided tongues, as of fire, and one sat upon each of them."[82] In each of these references, the fire of God *consumed* a particular object, place, or vessel, but it did not destroy it.

At Pentecost, the holy refining fire of God filled each of the disciples through the indwelling presence of His Spirit. When the Spirit of God consumes something or someone, an undeniable transformation occurs. Think of it this way—when you set something on fire, it causes a reaction that changes the

---

80   Genesis 1:3
81   Exodus 3:2
82   Acts 2:3

matter from one form to another. For example, from paper to ashes. The same applies when the Spirit of God consumes a person. A radical rearrangement of a spiritually molecular infrastructure occurs that causes a noticeable difference—or change—in the one being consumed. People who have been ignited by God become conduits of His presence and power. They become agents of change, capable of shifting any environment they find themselves in for the glory of God.

We witness a perfect example of this in Acts 28. The final chapter in this riveting book mentions the word *fire* three times in the first five verses. Paul experienced a very difficult voyage from Jerusalem in the previous chapter. His mission to Rome was delayed because of a shipwreck on the Mediterranean island of Malta. *Malta* is a word that means "honey." It was God's "sweet" response to the bitter trials Paul had endured on the way. Upon reaching the island, Paul and his crew were greeted by natives. Acts 28:2 says, "And the natives showed us unusual kindness; for they kindled a fire and made us all welcome, because of the rain that was falling and because of the cold." In those moments, fire represented warmth and light to a group of people who were weary from the turbulent storms at seas.

What happened next is important as it relates to the way God used Paul during his stay on Malta. Acts 28:3-5 says, "But when Paul had gathered a bundle of sticks and laid them on the fire, a viper came out because of the heat, and fastened on his hand. So when the natives saw the creature hanging from his hand, they said to one another, 'No doubt this man is a murderer, whom, though he has escaped the sea, yet justice does not allow to live.' But he shook off the creature into the fire and suffered no harm."

Notice the attack on Paul's life as soon as he decided to lend a helping hand. Notice also the reaction by the natives. They immediately judged and accused him. As you come to the end of this study in the book of Acts, it is critical that you understand the schemes of the enemy when you are moving forward in the work of the Lord. Sometimes, they are direct and blatant attacks from Satan on your life or health, such as the viper fastening onto Paul's hand. Other times, they are subtle and divisive attacks through others, such as the critical remarks made by the natives. In both cases, the intention is to break your spirit, invoke discouragement, and tempt you to give up—typically right before your breakthrough.

As you pursue the call of God on your life, there *will* be opposition. John 10:10 says, "The thief does not come except to steal, and to kill, and to destroy. I have come that they may have life, and that they may have it more abundantly." The thief has a job to do. The attacks *will* come, but Jesus promises victory and abundant life to all who call on His name. 1 John 4:4 says, "You are of God, little children, and have overcome them, because He who is in you is greater than he who is in the world."

Paul shook the viper off of his hand and suffered no harm. The power of God rendered him immune to the very assault that attempted to take his life. As a result, Acts 28:6 says, "However, they were expecting that he would swell up or suddenly fall down dead. But after they had looked for a long time and saw no harm come to him, they changed their minds and said that he was a god." The presence of God in your life will cause people to change their minds about you. It will open doors for you to reveal Him to others, and His favor will precede you everywhere you go.

> The presence of God in your life will cause people to change their minds about you.

Deuteronomy 9:3 says, "Therefore understand today that the Lord your God is He who goes over before you as a consuming fire. He will destroy them and bring them down before you; so you shall drive them out and destroy them quickly, as the Lord has said to you." The citizens of Malta were amazed by Paul's miraculous ability to resist death from the serpent's attack. God used this demonstration of power for Paul to perform many more signs and healing miracles on the island. None of this would have been possible if Paul had not been filled with the all-consuming fire of the Holy Spirit and been fully aware of his identity as a child of God. As he was leaving Malta, the natives who chastised him in the beginning were sending him off with honor and provision. Only God can effect a change like that!

The glory of God is reflected more and more in each of His children as the heat and pressure of life's trials increase. Acts 28:3 says, ". . . a viper came out because of the heat . . . ." One of the purposes of the fire of God is to refine you. His fiery presence abiding within you will convict, correct, and purify you. When the heat is on, evil will come out of the woodworks, so-to-speak. You will find yourself making decisions that will either cause you to look more like Christ or lead you further away from Him. You will occasionally face doubt and unbelief in your relationship with God. You will experience temptations and accusations from others aiming to deter you from the His will. Sometimes it may seem as though your provision is blocked or your mission has been sabotaged. In those moments, remember the Apostle Paul. Do not be surprised when the serpent of old, Satan, comes to steal, to kill, or to destroy just as you are about to enter your Promised Land. Instead, shake off the attack and continue to move in the direction God is calling you.

Genesis 50:20 says, "But as for you, you meant evil against me; but God meant it for good, in order to bring it about as it is this day, to save many people alive." The episode with the viper in Acts 28 was used by God to establish Paul's authority among the natives. It opened the door for him to pray for others on the island, healing their diseases and exalting the name of Jesus. The Lord knew that the people of Malta needed what Paul had to offer them. He allowed a "detour" on the way to Rome so Paul could set some captives free. God never says or does anything by accident. His leadership is perfect.

The book of Acts concludes with verses 28:30-31, "Then Paul dwelt two whole years in his own rented house, and received all who came to him, preaching the kingdom of God and teaching the things which concern the Lord Jesus Christ with all confidence, no one forbidding him." Imagine what was going on in the hearts of those who visited Paul during that time. Imagine the revival and awakening that must have taken place in their lives as a result of this man's faith and obedience. *Paul was a man on fire.* Wicked leaders, prison guards, unruly Jews, defiant unbelievers, and torrential rains could not quench this all-consuming fire in his life. His circumstances did not dictate his passion or his purpose. Paul lived intentionally for the glory of God. *He was rooted in his identity in Christ.* He knew who he was and what he was created to do. In all things and at all times, he maintained a burning zeal that was birthed out of His radical love for God. Chains could not hold him, storms could not suppress him, and Satan could not stop him. Jesus encountered him, Holy Spirit ignited him, and God used his obedience to change the world.

This is not only Paul's destiny. It is yours, and it is mine. The same Holy Spirit who consumed Paul's life wants to consume ours. He is simply waiting for willing submission to His divinely orchestrated plans and purposes. God is so much more powerful than we can imagine. We cannot comprehend Him with our finite minds. We must simply trust His word and believe, as Paul and so many others throughout the book of Acts did.

Say yes to Jesus. Respond to His call and set yourself apart. As you do, you will become a catalyst for change in every environment. His light radiating in and through you will impact your family, workplace, ministry, school, community, government, and the world. Prisoners will be set free as you surrender to His will and obey His voice. Go wherever He sends you and say whatever He tells you. Jesus is seeking souls who are lost and hurting. He wants you to be a conduit of His fiery presence, power, and love in their lives.

Think of yourself as a match. Once ignited, you have the potential to set everyone and everything around you on fire. Regardless of your age, gender, ethnicity, education, experience, or tenure as a Christian, God wants to use you to make a difference.

> *You are a firestarter.*

It is up to each of us to completely yield to the refining, all-consuming fire of the Holy Spirit in our lives. That is the only way we can truly live with passion and purpose.

You were created to burn with love for God. Wherever you go, whatever you do . . . *be the spark* that sets the world on fire for His glory.

Pause and Reflect

How has the book of Acts inspired you to live intentionally for the glory of God? What will you do to follow in the footsteps of the Apostles and do the greater works of which Jesus spoke?

_____

_____

_____

_____

_____

_____

_____

_____

_____

_____

Raw and Real

Like any other relationship, you have to fan the flame to keep the spark alive in your walk with God.

Short and Sweet

Spirit of God, set me on fire with Your burning love. I want to live purposefully and passionately like those who have gone before me in the book of Acts. I want to pick up where they left off, Lord, and change the world for Your glory. I wholly surrender to Your perfect will. I am Yours. Amen.

Meditate and Memorize

"But he shook off the creature into the fire and suffered no harm."
—Acts 28:5

Believe and Receive

All it takes is just one spark.

Listen and Learn
Ask God to set your heart on fire for Him.

Create and Relate
Use this space to connect with God through creativity.

Acts 29

This is not the end. It is a new beginning. I am not writing an additional chapter to the book of Acts. You are. *We are.* In this final exhortation, I want to encourage you and remind you of all that you have learned about God, yourself, and the followers of Christ in the book of Acts. Consider His great **LOVE** for you as you remember all that He has said and done through this Boot Camp Bible Study.

First, the God of the universe, the Father of creation, the all-knowing Being who dwells in eternal glory has ***chosen*** you for such a time as this. He wants you to be ***filled*** with the presence and power of His Holy Spirit so you can know your true identity in Christ. His great desire is that you be completely ***healed*** and made whole in your spirit, soul, and body. He has empowered you with ***boldness*** to accomplish all that He has called you to do and be in this life. One of your most blessed missions on earth is to know the ***truth*** and be set free by it. That requires an unshakable ***faith*** in who Jesus is and in who He says you are. Only then can you be an effective ***witness*** for Him and ***preach*** the gospel to every creature with confidence and zeal.

God has a ***vision*** for your life that He wants to release to you so you can do great and mighty things for His glory. ***Pray*** without ceasing and accept His ***grace*** as you pursue the purpose that has been assigned to you by your loving Father. It is time to ***arise***! The blood of Jesus has ***justified*** you! ***Turn*** from wickedness and experience a full ***conversion*** through the power of the Spirit and the holy sacrifice of the Lamb of God. As believers, we are all ***servants*** and ***offspring*** of the King of Glory! The ***occupation*** you choose will lead you to your Promised Land. ***Miracles***, signs, and wonders abound in that place. As a ***purchased disciple*** of Christ, your ***testimony*** of His love and faithfulness will set the multitudes free. Be of good ***cheer***! Your ***hope*** is in the Lord ***Jesus*** Christ! This is your great ***inheritance*** as a child of God. ***Believe*** His promises—every one is specifically for you. Let your ***fire*** burn brightly for all to see. The world is waiting for you, beloved.

Pause and Reflect

What will you do now to remain focused on the word of God and move forward in your purpose? How will you share what God has said and done in your life?

_____

_____

_____

_____

_____

_____

_____

_____

_____

_____

_____

_____

Raw and Real

The time to *act* is now.

Short and Sweet

Heavenly Father, thank You for Your strength and guidance. Thank You for the book of Acts and all that You have revealed to me through this study. Let this be the beginning of something new and powerful in my relationship with You. I long to know You more. Amen.

Meditate and Memorize

"The end of a thing is better than its beginning."
—Ecclesiastes 7:8

Believe and Receive

I can do all things through Christ.

Listen and Learn
Rejoice in your completion!

Create and Relate
Use this space to connect with God through creativity.

Epilogue

I remember as a new believer signing my name at the bottom of a blank piece of paper and telling the Lord, "Whatever it is, I say YES!" At the time, it was a heroic surrender to God's perfect will. Several years into my commitment, I realized that I had no idea what I was getting myself into. I initially thought I would lead armies into battle and conquer enemies with great victory like Joshua. I had grand visions of casting out demons and healing the sick as the multitudes gathered to hear the word of the Lord. I even imagined that I would part the waters—or at least the traffic—at some point in my journey (and I have tried!) Although I have tasted the goodness of God in miraculous and supernatural ways, the most beautiful encounters I have had with Him have been one-on-one in the secret place. He has mended my soul, healed my hurts, and delivered me from prisons I did not even know I was in. He has revealed His infinite love and power in my most desperate moments. He has released me from confusion and made a way where there seemed to be no way. He has continued to remind me that *He is good*. He is *always* good. My Father in heaven has given me the strength to carry on when all I wanted to do was give up, and He has taught me what it means to stand against all odds. He has shown me that I *can* do all things through Christ and that life without Him is not life at all.

Not long after the Lord revealed His purpose for my life, I specifically remember standing on a stump in a thicket overlooking a pond behind the subdivision where I lived. I was preaching my first sermon to "all of creation." The birds, bees, and creepy crawly critters were hearing a long-winded message about "Peace." At the end of my discourse, I picked up a staff . . . er, stick . . . and extended it over the water. With every bit of faith I could muster up, I commanded the waters to "Part! In the name of Jesus!" With nervous anticipation, I watched as the waters began to ripple and froth down the middle of the pond. In one terrifying second of hope and fear, I wondered what I would actually do if the Lord granted my request.

Needless to say, my faith completely disappeared in the midst of my analysis. The waters calmed, and my nerves did, too. In retrospect, I believe the Lord honored my childlike faith in those moments by giving me a tiny glimpse of His delight in my boldness. Although no one would have believed my story if the waters had actually piled up on both sides, that day stands as a constant reminder to me of how we, as Christians, often respond with doubt and unbelief to answered prayer.

The individuals of Acts 29 will be ones who do not doubt God's power or ability. We will be ones who are absolutely certain that He will move on our behalf because He loves us and desires to partner with us. We will be ones who have burning hearts of love for Him and others, provoking God to meet us in supernatural ways. Like those in the book of Acts who were used mightily by God, the disciples of Acts 29 will encounter Him because of their radical love, faith, and humility. This is when God will begin to part the waters and allow His people to experience "greater works."

God is waiting for your "YES!" At the end of this book, you will have an opportunity to sign your name at the bottom of a page that simply says "YES!" Let it serve as your commitment and surrender to an Almighty Creator who loves you and has great plans for your life. Join the **ACTS 29** family of believers whose hearts have been set ablaze by the presence and power of a loving God. Rest confidently in your identity and passionately pursue your purpose. Together we can pick up where the book of Acts left off. We can set hearts on fire and make a difference in the lives of people around the world. Remember, all it takes is *just one spark.*

Prayer

Abba Father, I thank You for the beautiful soul who dedicated this time to spend with You in the secret place. I ask You to bless Your child with all of the blessings of heaven and saturate Your beloved one with Your holy presence. I pray that each word that was studied would take root in the deep places, causing true transformation to occur in every way. I pray that Your will be done in Your servant's life, Lord, and that Your name be magnified every day. Thank You for the preparation of a heart for Your glory. I ask You for greater intimacy and a lifelong hunger for Your word for the one You call Your own. Lord, train Your disciple in all of Your ways. Keep the fire kindled, Holy Spirit, and provide strength for the journey. Allow the world to be forever changed because of a life well lived for Your honor and glory. Let it be so in the mighty and perfect name of Jesus Christ of Nazareth. Amen.

God's greatest blessings in abundance, Mighty Warrior!
Congratulations on completing this Boot Camp Bible Study.

"A fire shall always be burning on the altar;
it shall never go out."
Leviticus 6:13

Kindle the Fire

Affirmations

God picked me.
God wants to fill me with Himself.
God still heals.
I am bold as a lion.
I will speak the truth at all times.
I am full of faith and the Holy Spirit.
My body is a temple.
I am called to preach.
I once was blind, but now I see.
Prayer is a priority in my life.
God's grace is sufficient for me.
The truth will make me free.
God sees me through the blood of Jesus.
I will turn from useless things.
I am a new creation.
I am a servant of the Most High God.
I am a child of God.
God blesses the work of my hands.
Miracles are real.
Jesus died for *me*.
I am a disciple of Christ.
I will share my testimony with others.
The joy of the Lord is my strength.
My hope is *in* Christ.
Jesus is the name above every name.
Everything that is His is mine.
I believe.
All it takes is just one spark.
I can do all things through Christ.

Kindle the Fire

Confession

I am **chosen** by God, **filled** with His Spirit, and **healed** by His love. I have been given **boldness** to speak the **truth**. I will live by **faith**, as a **witness** of His everlasting love and sacrifice. I am called to **preach** Christ and Him crucified to a lost and dying world. God has a life-changing, earth-shaking **vision** for my life. I will **pray** without ceasing and accept His **grace** every day as I pursue His heart for me and for others. It is my time to **arise**! I have been **justified** before a holy God by the blood of the Lamb. I will **turn** to Him in all of my ways. I will allow my **conversion** to be an example of God's power to change wicked people into devoted **servants**. I am a child of God, His beloved **offspring**. The **occupation** of my Promised Land will release **miracles** into the earth for His glory. I am a **purchased disciple** of Christ. I will share my **testimony** with great **cheer** and abounding **hope**. **Jesus** is my glorious **inheritance**! I **believe** I will set hearts and lives on **fire** as I **act** according to His word and fulfill my destiny in the earth.

Amen

YES!

_____

Signature

_____

Date

References

Scriptures taken from the New King James Version®.
Copyright © 1982 by Thomas Nelson, Inc.
Used by permission. All rights reserved.

Strong, James. Strong's Complete Word Study Concordance.
Ed. Warren Baker. Chattanooga: AMG Publishers, 2004.

Meyers, Rick. e-Sword Bible Study Software.
Copyright © 2012. All rights reserved worldwide.
<http://www.e-sword.net>.

Olive Tree Bible Software. Copyright © 1983-2013.
<http://www.olivetree.com>.

Dictionary.com LLC. Copyright © 2013. <http://dictionary.com>.